MW01281989

MY DAUGHTER, HER SUICIDE, AND GOD

MY DAUGHTER, HER SUICIDE, AND GOD

A Memoir of Hope

MARJORIE ANTUS

ISBN: 1501041185

ISBN 13: 9781501041181

For Mary

CONTENTS

FOREWORD

IN MARCH 2014, I RECEIVED a letter from Marjorie Antus asking if I would be willing to write a Foreword to her book *My Daughter, Her Suicide, and God: A Memoir of Hope.* I called her promptly and said that I would be happy to do so. However, when I hung up the phone, I had second thoughts. Who was I to comment on the feelings of a mother whose teenage daughter had died by suicide? I'm a Roman Catholic priest. I have never been married nor had children of my own. How could I comment on her grief? How could I *enter into* this book? The answer was simple: I couldn't. Nevertheless, I found myself *being drawn* into it.

What drew me into the text was the utter candor of the author. As she chronicles the events following the suicide of her daughter Mary, Marjorie reveals her inner feelings. The text is written on two levels. On the surface, Marjorie presents us with her social persona, what society expected her to say and do in certain situations. However, beneath the conventions of propriety, she reveals what she was thinking and feeling by use of italics. As I read the text, I repeatedly found myself saying, "Yes, that's what I would think; that's how I would feel in this situation." Let us take a couple of examples.

At her daughter's wake, people came up to Marjorie to offer their condolences.

> "Your daughter is in a better place," many said. *What was the matter with this place? And what better place is she supposed to have gone to, and how could she have gone there ahead of me?*

Is there anyone who, during a time of grief, hasn't felt anger at someone's words of consolation? I remember attending the funeral of a young girl named Alice. In his homily, the priest said, "This world is God's garden and when God walks through it, he picks the most beautiful flowers for himself. God has picked little Alice to adorn his palace." I shook my head in disbelief. *I can't believe he said that with Alice's parents sitting there.* However, were there *any* words that the priest could have said to comfort Alice's parents? In the face of deep grief, words of consolation are often powerless to console.

I'm reminded of C. S. Lewis's statement when he was mourning the death of his wife, Joy, and people were offering him consolation.

> Talk to me about the truth of religion and I'll listen gladly. Talk to me about the duty of religion and I'll listen submissively.
>
> But don't come talking to me about the consolations of religion or I shall suspect that you don't understand.[1]

To cite another example, the Sunday after Mary's funeral, when Marjorie and her family attended Mass, the following incident happened.

> At communion, I couldn't keep back tears when Father Jack placed the Eucharist in my hand. Colleen,

sitting directly behind us, wept into her handkerchief, and I sensed that dozens of people throughout the church were praying for us by name. Just the same, when glowing pregnant women and their husbands came forward after Mass for a special blessing, it was not warmth I was feeling but bitterness. *You're going to have your hearts broken too. You just don't know it yet.*

The thoughts and feelings that arose from the author's grief are understandably raw and bitter; yet, they can prove to be a great blessing to all of us. They offer us permission to think and feel the same way that she did without feeling either ashamed or guilty.

Although Marjorie realized that her emotions were commensurate with her grief, she also knew that in order to come to peace, she had to reconcile Mary's suicide with her religious beliefs. In consequence, she decided to continue on a course of study at Washington Theological Union. Her studies provided her with a framework to think about her daughter's suicide, and writing her master's thesis on suicide and the Catholic community was a healing experience. However, the deep wounds of life are never completely healed. The author faced the question that all of us face when we are confronted with tragedy. How does one go on living, knowing that life will never be the same again?

Marjorie framed this question within her experience of being torn between two great needs, what she labels as *A* issues and *B* issues. *A* issues refer to her need to come to grips with all the unanswered questions and unresolved emotions surrounding Mary's suicide. *B* issues refer to attending to the needs of her husband and her two emotionally fragile children. How does one attend to the needs of others while a strong force is pulling one inward to deal with one's own pain? Isn't this one of the great challenges in life for all of us?

During the defense of her master's thesis on suicide and the Catholic community, one of the professors asked Marjorie, "Where's the resurrection in this thesis?" She pointed to her heart and said, "It's right here." This is where all of us find hope in the resurrected Christ in our lives, in a broken heart struggling to be healed.

This reality is portrayed in Piero della Francesca's painting *The Resurrection*. It is daybreak, the moment between night and day. Christ's right leg is *in* the grave and in the background on his right side are the barren trees of winter. His left leg is on the cover of the sarcophagus and in the background on his left side are the budding trees of spring. In the center of the painting is the risen Christ, holding in his wounded hand, the banner of victory. The painting suggests that this is where all of us experience the resurrected Christ: in the intersection between winter and spring; between sorrow and joy; at daybreak, betwixt night and day.

The author does not conclude by offering readers the false hope that one can completely "work through" or come to a resolution on the great losses in life. Nevertheless, *My Daughter, Her Suicide, and God: A Memoir of Hope* is a book of hope because it tells us that the resurrected Christ is present in the midst of the pain and the obdurate questions attending inexplicable loss.

Marc Foley, O.C.D.
Washington, D.C.
April 7, 2014

Endnote

1 C. S. Lewis, *A Grief Observed* (New York: Bantam Books, 1976), 28.

PREFACE

THIS BOOK BEGAN IN CONFUSION. When I sat down on the night of August 17, 2001, to begin writing, I had no clear sense whom I was writing for and no indication that anyone would want to read a mother's story about the suicide of her seventeen-year-old daughter. I did know that I had to write it. Six years after my daughter Mary's death, I felt an urgency to describe how I had lived with it over the years. I wanted to impose order on an inherently disorderly and devastating act. I wanted peace.

From time to time during the decade of writing, people asked how the manuscript was going. I usually ended up saying, "I'm compelled to write it." But that wasn't true. Compelled would have meant that I was being urged to write by someone or something outside of me, but nothing and no one was urging such a thing. Those closest to me hinted that the project would reopen a barely healed wound and burden me unnecessarily. At best—and this is the most anyone seemed to envision—it might provide a kind of therapy: a catharsis, a psychological freedom.

Yet, the desire to write was coming from within that August night; and I believe it was coming from God, who was impelling me to put pain on paper and see what I could make of it. Despite my utter bafflement at Mary's suicide, I had always believed that God was with her as she began overdosing on her antidepressant medication. I had also personally sensed God's mysterious nearness throughout my grieving years. So on that summer night in 2001, I felt I was finally ready to begin a story about suicide and God.

What about my daughter? She had done violence to herself and left her family in the night without saying goodbye: a terrible disruption of everything dear and meaningful in our lives together. I had yearned all along to repair our broken relationship and finally realized that my only remedy was to write Mary back into being.

There is still one more reason for telling this story about my daughter: it bears witness to her beautiful life and refuses to let suicide be its last word.

1

FINDING AND LOSING

In the noontime of life I must depart.
ISAIAH 38:10[1]

MY SON WAS THE LAST person to see her. Around eleven o'clock on Saturday night, he saw Mary watching a comedy show on the basement television and eating a bowl of ice cream. He said that when he walked through the room, she was actually laughing. He remembered her saying, "Watch this, John Paul. It's funny."

So he stood with her for a moment and watched the show before wandering off to bed. An hour or so later—when the doors had been locked and lights turned off, when my husband John and I had finished viewing *A Man for All Seasons* and gone to sleep, when the house was finally quiet—sometime around then, Mary got up from her chair and went to an old basement refrigerator. She took out a bottle of champagne and carried it upstairs to her bedroom.

Slipping out of her sandals and jeans, she showered, picked up her bottle of antidepressant medication from the bathroom cabinet, and returned to her room. She locked the door and applied makeup, then put on the flowing black dress she had worn to her prom five months before.

She found photographs of her friends and spread them on the floor at the foot of her bed, located a favorite pen, dug her physics notebook out of a pile on her desk, poured the pills into her hand to count them, popped the champagne cork, and sat down on the floor to write her note. Penning "Sept. 24 '95, 12:40 a.m." at the top of the page, she began: "So, how do you write yourself out of this world?" She wrote that she'd always considered suicide to be "darkly mystical" especially when the victim was young and the death shocking. "How romantic—to suffer in silence."

Mary described how her recent days had unfolded: "Each night I go to bed trying to forget that today happened and hoping I won't wake up for tomorrow." In the hallways of her high school she had wondered, "What am I doing here? I don't understand how other kids think and what they laugh at. I don't even know when to laugh or why anyone would want to." That was all she could say. It wasn't much of a reason for choosing to die, plenty of people were much worse off, but she couldn't bear her life another day.

She said her family had been good to her, and she allowed that her death would cause pain and anger. Writing "I'm sorry" four times, she said her death was no one's fault and that her family was not to be blamed. "There's no way that this won't hurt you all, so I won't say, 'Don't be hurt.' I will say, 'Please forgive me.' I am selfish and thoughtless. Pray for my soul." She asked family members to be gentle with each other and remember her good moments.

Tapping out several dozen pills, she began taking them a couple at a time, washing them down with sips of champagne to heighten their tranquillizing effect. From experience, she knew their potency. She knew that even two pills would make her sleep several hours, so once she started swallowing them, there was no turning back. Everything would be ruined if she only half completed the job and ended up not dead but in a coma for the rest of her life.

After thirty minutes, all the pills were gone and she was feeling woozy, but she added, "I finally had the guts to do *something* decisive." After an apology to John Paul—"You're so sweet and gentle and caring. You deserve the best"—she said it was just like her "to keep writing and not say anything worth a damn—the story of my life." Once more she apologized to all the people she'd hurt and ended with, "I was weak, and I hated myself." She put down her pen, staggered into bed, and turned off the bedside lamp. It was 1:30 a.m. Two and a half hours had passed since the ice cream, the comedy show, and the laughter.

On that night, I was immersed in suburban family life, having stepped away from teaching English to high-school students in 1974 when John Paul was born. Twenty years of being at home with children, while demanding, had been the best years: the richest, most creative and fun years of my life. I got to be around the kids all the time and run the house pretty much as I pleased while John tended to his medical practice as a general internist. When John's older patients asked what it was like being married to the "doc," I felt they were trying to thank me for putting up with late dinners and late phone calls, so I answered, "It's fine," because it was.

Part of life's fineness stemmed from a parenting principle we thought had served pretty well: if John and I kept our priorities straight, we could know and do the right thing most of the time for our children. If we did the right things in the right way for them, we could keep them safe, and that was the point— their safety. I was gauging safety by my experience as a child growing up in the 1950s on the outskirts of Richmond, Virginia: hopscotch after church in the noonday sun while my parents chatted with friends, fried chicken Sunday dinners, open-ended Sabbath afternoon tranquility. I honestly believed, or at least hoped, that John and I could make our children secure in their world with such innocent family togetherness.

Still, I was asleep when the champagne cork popped into Mary's ceiling on the last night of her life. I heard nothing unusual that night or the next morning when I woke at 6:30. The house was steeped in darkness on what seemed an ordinary Sunday morning. When I passed Mary's door at 8:00, there was no sound coming from her room, so there was no reason to turn the doorknob and peek in. After walking past Mary's door, I woke John Paul, who had asked me the night before to wake him so he could study.

When John and I left the house that morning to spend the day in prayer at a Carmelite monastery, it wasn't as though we hadn't been schooled in the ways of mental illness and, to a certain extent, teen suicide. In one sense, everyone in our family had been coping with mental illness for several years, beginning in 1991 when John Paul, then seventeen, started withdrawing from family gatherings. I remember him sitting with his head down at the Christmas dinner table that year. During dessert, he didn't join in the laughter with relatives but got up without a word and slipped out to shoot baskets in the cold December air. That was an unusual thing for him to do, but I wrote it off as teenage moodiness.

One evening in late January when I was fixing dinner, John Paul followed me around the kitchen, talking animatedly about his life. His new openness was amusing right up to the point where he said he was a nervous wreck and didn't want to go to school. That admission got me to take off the oven mitt, sit down, and look into my son's worried brown eyes. His monologue about a girl he liked was hard to follow, even incoherent, disturbingly unlike any speech pattern he'd ever used.

He said, "Ginger's calf muscle is shaped like mine, so we're supposed to be together." Not knowing what to make of that, I nevertheless didn't immediately assume my son was on drugs; and even John tried to call the changes in John Paul normal. What we weren't seeing, though, was the wobble in his classroom performance and the drop in his grades.

By early February, John had decided our son needed both a physical examination and a psychiatric evaluation. The physical exam made sense to me, but a psychiatrist? That John Paul might be mentally ill stunned me, and I was unprepared to hear the psychiatrist say, "I think he's borderline psychotic." Suddenly, we were living in the realm of drug tests, psychological tests, brain scans, and finally, antipsychotic medication and psychotherapy. On some level, Mary and her younger sister, Lauren, were drawn into the gloom of their brother's illness, but because it wasn't something either of them spoke about, I didn't know—I still don't know—the impact of his infirmity on their sense of well-being. I do know fear and grief stole into our family and took up residence.

JOHN PAUL WITH MARY AND LAUREN ON THE NIGHT BEFORE
HE LEFT FOR THE UNIVERSITY OF MIAMI, 1993.

Two years later, in 1994, the notions of "son" and "suicide" collided in my mind for the first time. Up to that point, John Paul seemed to have regained stability. He had graduated from high school with honors and entered the University of Miami where he was enrolled in his third semester. But we didn't know he'd stopped taking his antipsychotic medication a few weeks into the semester and become restless and disorganized. One November night, his psychiatrist called to say she'd gone looking for him on campus after he missed an appointment with her. "I had to find him. When students stop taking their medication, they can get desperate and jump off buildings," she told us.

Jump off buildings? My son, jump off a building? No experience I'd ever had prepared me to consider such a thing; fortunately, we were spared that autumn. John Paul did not jump off a building; he came home to us for good after spending a week in a Miami hospital psychiatric unit. But the idea of suicide wormed its way into my family.

In setting out for the monastery that September Sunday morning in 1995, John and I were seeking a few hours of prayerful silence in the community of other people. We left the house for eight critical hours that day because we're secular Carmelites, Catholics living in the world who agree to pray silently twice a day. In becoming members of the community six years before, John and I had also agreed to attend community meetings once a month at the Discalced Carmelite monastery on Lincoln Road in Washington, D.C.

Our intention was not to escape daily routine but to enter into it more deeply through prayer, so leaving our house that morning, leaving our calm home and doomed daughter, was tied up with love for our children and each other. Truly, it was John Paul who seemed most to need our prayer that day. Enrolled at nearby George Mason University, he had lately been paralyzed by anxiety whenever he tried to study; and I was dreading the possibility that he might not ever finish college.

As we neared the monastery just before 9 a.m., an odd thing happened: John's cell phone rang. In six years of monastery visits, that had never happened because of the weekend patient coverage he always coordinated with other doctors. On that morning, however, an emergency call came through that made John think about turning the car around and heading home where, before leaving for the hospital, he would have dropped me off around 10:00. An hour later, I would've knocked on Mary's door to wake her for the noon Mass. The frenzy would have begun.

John decided that the doctor on call could take care of the patient and that we should go on to the monastery where, as it turned out, we were given a few peaceful hours before the coming chaos. We were given what St. Teresa of Avila had given her Carmelite nuns in sixteenth-century Spain: a place to pray as Christ's friends for the good of the church and world.

As we drew near the monastery we passed St. Mary's Catholic Cemetery, an expanse filled with worn headstones and vaults like tiny angel-adorned houses. The rows of granite on that cemetery lawn always draw my eye and add seriousness to the monastery day—as if more were needed.

In the hush of the friars' chapel that Sunday, John and I took our place in the second pew and began chanting Psalm 95 from the morning Liturgy of the Hours. "Come let us sing to the Lord and shout with joy to the Rock who saves us."[2] Like everyone else, I knew the verses by heart. Over the years, they had urged me to praise God in the worst moments, or at least not to condemn God in the worst moments. Like everyone else, I was praying not just for my intentions but for those of the entire church. Without the vaguest notion of it, our chant was sanctifying not only that particular moment of the day but also the hour of Mary's demise.

It was now 9:30 a.m., and eight hours had passed since our daughter had climbed into bed and turned out her lamp. During a gathering song, two dozen of us, mostly women—teachers and nurses, librarians and social workers, accountants and retired federal employees---stood as Father Kieran processed down the aisle.

It was turning out to be a typical, low-key liturgy. While reading aloud from the prophet Amos, for example, Cynthia had to cast her voice over the crackle of Pauline's paper lunch bag opening and closing: "Hear this, you who trample upon the needy and destroy the poor of the land!"[3] And just as Father Kieran was urging us to pray for the desire to be holy, the organist accidentally put her elbow on the keyboard and produced a rogue chord, which brought smiles.

In its humanity, ours was a divine gathering with Eucharist at its center—fruit of the earth come down from heaven and held aloft by Father Kieran. While walking down the aisle toward him for communion, I tried to make myself present to Presence itself, the mystery of grace that took us to the upper room on the night before Jesus died and brought the upper room to our plain chapel. Placed in my hand was Life itself not only for me but also for John and our family.

After Mass, we all prayed silently for half an hour, ate sandwiches in the monastery dining room, sat for a presentation about Carmelite spirituality, and conducted community business, all with a good amount of laughter before saying good-bye.

It was an uncomplicated day and a refreshing one. Upon arriving home at three-thirty that afternoon, I saw *The Washington Post* lying at the bottom of the driveway and wondered why Mary hadn't picked it up as she usually did. The first thing I asked John Paul was, "Where's Mary?"

"Taking a nap." When I checked on her and found a locked door and soundless room, I knew something was terribly wrong. As I started calling, "Mary!" and pounding on her door, John raced up the stairs, put his shoulder to the door and forced his way into the room. There, Mary lay on the bed in her black prom dress, her head bobbing rhythmically to the right, her eyes closed.

"What's wrong with her?" I stepped over a champagne bottle, rushed around the bed, and turned on the bedside lamp. John knew right away what was wrong.

"She's having a seizure. Grand mal."

"Mary!" It was all I could say: a plea to open her eyes and speak.

"She can't hear you," John said. And part of me knew she was beyond anything I could say or do, far beyond me in another reality. Incongruous thoughts came rushing in: *What a stupid thing to do. . . . So this is what she's been trying to tell us . . . She's hurt herself so badly . . . Just what do you think you're doing, Mary?* My customary way of dealing with misbehavior was now obsolete; words of disapproval would not make her sit up and come to her senses. Mary and I were both helpless.

John sat on the bed and lifted Mary into his arms. "Oh, my darling, . . . you've got a pulse and you're still breathing." He cleared her airway and began cardiopulmonary resuscitation.

I stared at what lay on the floor: a half-consumed bottle of Korbel Brut along with a school notebook, pictures of her friends, and an empty pill container that had held her anti-depressant. *Empty.* What I was seeing—the prom dress, the champagne—was a weird celebration of her death and not an accidental overdose. She swallowed all the medication she had on hand; it was clear she meant to die.

"What did she take?" John asked.

"Nortriptyline—the whole bottle."

"Not good, not good . . . that's a lethal dose. Go call 911!"

"What do I say?"

"Tell them she's having a seizure." We couldn't yet say "suicide." In hurrying to our bedroom telephone, I caught my shoe on a piece of underwear lying on the floor and kicked it across the room. All I wanted was to make the 911 call, get the help, and go back to Mary. Returning to her bedroom, I leaned over to see her face, and in that instant, my long good-bye began: *Oh God, her mouth is blue! She's gone, and I will never have my lovely living daughter back again.*

Even if her heart could be kept beating, Mary's life—her dearness, intelligence, sensitivity, beauty—was over. The most I could hope for was a brain-damaged daughter on a ventilator for the rest of her days. Without anyone telling me that, I knew it. Mary's life was over; and in a manner and at a depth I have never been able to fathom, my life was also over.

My sister, Joy, lives next door and, at that time, my mother lived on the next block. After calling 911, I phoned my mother. "Something horrible has happened. Mary tried to commit suicide," I told her, and she instantly broke into tears.

By the time I went downstairs to unlock the door for the rescue squad, Joy had run across the yard. Clearly startled, she told me about a friend who as a teen overdosed and survived to live a good life. "Just hold onto that," she said.

I appreciated her optimism but also grasped the difference between her perspective and mine: she had not seen Mary's face, and I had. Mary wanted to die and was, in fact, dying. She had violated herself, she had violated me, she had violated everyone who knew her.

Four men in dark uniforms, the rescue squad, rushed in, juggling a gurney and heart monitor along with several slender black containers holding intravenous bags, poles, and tubing. I followed the crew to Mary's bedroom where they cut the prom dress off her, placed her on the floor, and began hooking her up to the monitor. John loomed over them, necktie hanging loose, speaking rapidly. The space was too small for seven people, so I retreated to the doorway and my own jumbled denials: *Why is Mary lying naked on the floor? What are these strangers doing in her room, and why am I allowing them to look at her? How did our nice Sunday afternoon end up like this?*

One man said on his cell phone, "Tell them we have an 'S' here." It didn't occur to me he might mean seizure as I'd told the 911 operator. "S" could only mean suicide. *He thinks I'll lose control if I hear the word.* But there would be no outbursts from me. I was subdued and humiliated, not hysterical. Going into my bedroom, I sat on the bed with John Paul and wailed, "What happened?"

"She was in her room all day, Mom. I thought she was asleep. I was downstairs watching the Redskins . . . I don't know." His eyes were full of fear.

"Listen, this isn't your fault. Mary's the one who did this. You had nothing to do with it. So nobody's blaming you, okay?"

"Okay."

I walked around the bedroom asking myself whether anyone had argued with her. Had anyone hurt her feelings? The answer that kept coming back was no; she'd taken those pills for no apparent reason. As much as I hurt for my daughter, I started distancing myself from her and putting together my defense: *I thought she was better, I really did. She never used the word "suicide" around me; she was receiving good medical care. How was I supposed to know?*

When the police detective arrived a few minutes later, I realized what had taken place in our home was a crime for which we were going to be questioned. It was insulting, the whole rigmarole, and I blamed Mary for putting us through it. The detective followed John Paul into his bedroom where God alone knew what he would say.

My mother and Tom, Joy's husband, were standing around downstairs. There were no tears that I could see, only anxious waiting, pacing, and practically nothing to say. An obstetrician from the neighborhood named Charles walked in and asked if he could help, but after seeing the rescue squad he came back downstairs and asked, "What happened?"

"My daughter tried to kill herself," I said. Mary's suicide attempt became public at that instant. Because I didn't have the wits or will to cover it up, anyone who wanted to know the truth could know the truth. I had a feeling the truth would set us free or at least bring us help, and the feeling proved to be accurate. "Would you like me to call the rectory at All Saints and let them know?" Charles asked.

"Would you?" The priest on call would know how much trouble Mary was in and would hasten to the emergency room and anoint her with sacramental oil. That I could count on.

A few minutes later, the gurney on which Mary lay was carried down the stairs and out the front door. Covered to her neck by a white sheet, she lay on her back in the sun of a late

September afternoon. "That's my baby out there," I said to my mother who gazed at me, wordless. "At least her color is a little better. At least she's a little whiter now."

Tom drove John and me to the hospital. When we arrived, the gurney was being hauled from the back of the rumbling truck amid the stench of diesel fumes. I studied Mary's face as she went by, but her safekeeping was entirely out of my hands, it had been out of my hands for some time without my knowing it, and all I could see were her closed eyes and the oxygen cup over her nose. A middle-aged woman took me by the arm, guided John and me into the waiting room and said, "You need to understand your daughter will receive the best possible care, okay?" Then she backed out and shut the door.

"She's afraid we're going to make a scene, isn't she?" I said. Neither John nor I had any intention of going into the emergency room. What we had to do was sit and pray. We prayed aloud as never before, our words surging with fear. I didn't expect Mary to live. I didn't think God would intervene and restore her damaged heart and brain. But I prayed hard for it.

Our eleven-year-old daughter, Lauren, had been visiting a friend over the weekend. Calling home, I learned that as soon as Lauren arrived, Joy took her aside and said, "Mary tried to hurt herself; she's at the hospital." What would that sound like to a child? John and I took turns telling Lauren all that the medical team was doing. Several times she said, "Okay," in a soft voice. I hung up, relieved she was safe with my family and hadn't cried or asked why.

Father Dave, from All Saints Parish, tapped on the door and walked in. A pleasant-looking man with a quick smile under normal conditions, his face was blank. "I just anointed her feet," he said. "That was the only part of her body not being worked on." Without another word, he sat down. By blessing Mary with healing oil, he had already convened the entire faith community around her. He himself was a sign of hope.

John began pouring out the day's events to Father Dave, which hadn't seemed like events until I heard them recounted in that edgy waiting room. I chimed in about all the praying we had done at the monastery, wanting him to understand that no matter how oblivious to Mary's distress John and I had been, at least we were spending the last hours of her life worthily. But it was nonsense. There was no getting around the image of Mary developing in my mind: a dejected child sitting on her bedroom floor taking deadly pills. During those Sunday hours that I was surrounded by people, Mary was radically alone, or felt herself to be. How in the name of God was I ever going to live with that?

In the commotion of the rescue attempt an hour earlier, we hadn't read her suicide note and were left guessing. What set Mary off on her downward spiral that particular September day? Had she taken the pills after we left the house? Was she angry at us for leaving her? Had she thought we could withstand her death for having spent the day in prayer? Father Dave listened, seemingly free of the need to make sense of the situation.

Dr. Matthews, the psychiatrist to whom we'd entrusted not only John Paul but also Mary, appeared at the door wearing weekend cookout clothes, having just left a family gathering as soon as John phoned. She hugged me like a mother. "It doesn't look good," I whispered. "It doesn't look good."

"I am so very sorry," she said, taking a seat with us in our little anxiety chamber. "Why did I ever prescribe that medication, and so much of it? I'll never prescribe it again, I can tell you that." It was a strikingly unguarded admission, the likes of which I didn't expect to hear from her again.

"Nancy, I've always considered you a model for my own prescribing," John said.

"Oh, please . . . ," she said with a flick of her hand.

But I could see John wasn't going to blame Dr. Matthews for what Mary had done. It would have been out of character for him to accuse a doctor he considered well-intentioned. It also would have been out of keeping with reality. In fact, our daughter went behind a locked door and emptied the contents of a pill container down her throat. She might not have *been* herself in that locked room, but whoever that self was swallowed those pills. No one made her do it. That was the truth, a very hard one that, following John's example, I had to acknowledge in principle even as I was recoiling from it.

Minutes dragged by. Like a child sent to her room, I awaited the authoritative footsteps, the opening of the door, the punishment. I fiddled with a button on my skirt, thinking all the while that cardiologists, anesthesiologists, nurses, and medical technicians who never knew Mary valued her life more than she valued it herself. "Why don't you go see what's happening?" I asked John.

"No. I need to stay out of there." John could have watched his colleagues work on Mary but chose not to, sensing that he'd done all he could do.

The emergency room doctor came in to tell us, "We're making some headway getting a heart rhythm." Then a clerk brought us a card with a hospital room number assigned to Mary, a practicality that made me think someone out there must have hope. Father Dave left the waiting room and came back to say that the doctors wanted to transport Mary by helicopter to Fairfax Hospital for dialysis. "But," he added, "for them to do that,

she needs to have a blood pressure, and she doesn't have one."
*God—no blood pressure. She's not coming back. It's over, it's hopeless,
she's gone.*

John and I talked about our last day with Mary. As if to latch
onto something real, I showed a cut on my palm which I'd gotten
the day before when I'd fallen in the street while jogging. I told
them that when I limped into the kitchen on a throbbing ankle,
Mary brought me an ice pack for it, and she also said that she'd
go to the grocery store later if I needed her to. I wanted Father
Dave and Dr. Matthews to know that Mary seemed normal the
day before her death, and not only normal but also tender. I
wanted everyone to know she had cared about me. But stealing
through me was a sadness I kept to myself: *This is the last afternoon I'll ever be able to start a sentence with "Yesterday, Mary said . . ."*

John told how Mary helped him clear away the Saturday dinner dishes, and I recalled that, while she picked over steak and
carrots and didn't seem hungry, she came up with a quick comment that got us laughing.

"It's amazing how you can be eating dinner with someone
and have no idea what they're thinking," John said. He added
that he'd invited Mary to jog through the neighborhood with
him after dinner and that she'd declined.

I told them I called down to the basement where she was
watching television to ask if she wanted to see *A Man for All
Seasons* but that she replied, "No thanks, I'm watching something right now." Those were the last words I ever heard her
say, and now I was repeating them with the polite airiness I had
heard in her voice. Perhaps out of consideration, Mary wanted
to make her final words pleasant. More likely, she was just dis-
guising her desperation.

The emergency room doctor, whose surgical scrubs were streaked with blood, finally opened the door. He explained that Mary's lungs were full of fluid, a condition that could not be remedied. Through tears, he said, "John, I'm sorry. If there's anything I can do, you let me know." *Wait a minute . . . is he telling us she's dead?* When he closed the door, the four of us rose from our chairs and embraced. The others wept, but I cursed the helplessness of it. Father Dave suggested we sit for a minute to pray, and then he read aloud a Prayer of Commendation of the Dying:

> Go forth, Christian soul, from this world in the name
> of God the almighty Father, who created you, in the
> name of Jesus Christ, Son of the living God, who suf-
> fered for you, in the name of the Holy Spirit, who was
> poured out upon you, go forth, faithful Christian.
> May you live in peace this day, may your home be
> with God in Zion, with Mary, the virgin Mother of
> God, with Joseph, and all the angels and saints.[4]

With those words, Mary's death became official. The child of my womb had stepped forth from this world into an eternity I could not comprehend. I was terrified. *She's gone from me; she's on her own with God.* I held fast to one thing: Hadn't Father Dave called her "Christian"? Had he not sent her forth in the name of the Father, Son, and Holy Spirit?

Dr. Matthews told John and me we ought to say good-bye. She said if we didn't do so, we would regret it. *Good-bye? What good is that? She's dead.* I motioned for her to come with me to the area where Mary lay connected to tubes with a suction device pumping bloody fluid from her lungs. John went ahead of us, raised Mary's eyelid, observed her fixed, dilated pupil, and rushed out in tears.

As I approached my daughter, Dr. Matthews stepped back to allow privacy; but privacy was not what I needed. I was oblivious to everything around me, enclosed with Mary in another universe at the edge of time. What I needed was to get hold of the scene before my eyes, to understand it for what it was, to touch Mary, and to get away. Blood was dripping on the floor underneath her table, and I crouched to see where it was coming from but couldn't figure it out. I did notice a red pinch mark on her right hip and thought how much it would have hurt had she been able to feel. I picked up her right arm, it was still warm, and I caressed it. Nine months before, she had one day taken a razor blade to that arm and cut half-inch slits from her wrist to her elbow. Now no more than small white lines on pink flesh, they dared me not to forget her anguish.

Dr. Matthews and I walked away from Mary's gurney with our arms around each other. "I'm so sorry for prescribing that medication," Dr. Matthews said. "I cannot believe . . ."

"Even without the pills, she probably would have found a way." Mary's determination to die shocked and repelled me. She'd pushed free will to the limit and no one, not even God, could stop her. *She probably would have found another way.*

When my brother-in-law Tom joined John and me in the corridor, the only thing he asked was which door we wanted to use in exiting the hospital. In a haze I said, "We'll just follow you." Stepping out onto the portico where I had stood nearly eighteen years before with my newborn Mary, I said inanely (as though to tidy up the mess), "She was born on a Sunday, and she died on a Sunday."

I've wanted almost ever since to tell her story, and mine, which together make a kind of love story.

Endnotes

1 Isaiah 38:10, *Christian Prayer: The Liturgy of the Hours* (New York: Catholic Book Publishing Co., 1976), 1488.

2 Psalm 95:1, *Christian Prayer: The Liturgy of the Hours* (New York: Catholic Book Publishing Co., 1976), 688.

3 Amos 8:4, *The Roman Missal: Lectionary for Mass* (New York: Catholic Book Publishing Co., 1970), 224.

4 Prayer of Commendation of the Dying, *Pastoral Care of the Sick: Rites of Anointing and Viaticum* (New York: Catholic Book Publishing Co., 1983), 206-7.

2

GATHERING

*No one has ever seen God. Yet if we love one another
God dwells in us, and his love is brought to perfection in us.*
1 JOHN 4:12[5]

THE STRANGEST OF ALL WEEKS had begun. I climbed into the back seat of Tom's car, so clean and orderly, and fastened my seat belt as if there were something left of me worth protecting. John turned to Tom in the front seat and said, "I know you've been through some hellish moments with your own kids."

"But there are degrees of hell," Tom said. *Right, and we're at the highest degree.*

Hell was the thought of Mary's face covered with a sheet. Hell was the hollowness inside my chest. I had experienced something of God's nearness at Carmel a few hours earlier. But that nearness had vanished, and in my homeward ride, there was no peace that passes understanding and no inner reassuring voice. There was only the silence.

Even without reading the suicide note, I had a feel for what Mary had done. It was the "why" that stupefied me, and along with that problem came others. How were we supposed to live without her? Who was she, and how could John and I not have known who she was? What was taking place between her and God? And where *was* God, anyway? Answers, such as they were, lay years in the future.

As we approached the house, I saw how quickly word had traveled within my family: the driveway was full of cars. Parked in front of the house, a blue police cruiser signaled to the world that something illegal had taken place.

"What's that cop still doing here?" I asked without expecting a reply. As John walked across the lawn to talk with Dr. Anderson, my parents' pastor, I made my way up the driveway.

My sister-in-law Rita, niece Kristine, and nephew Hudson had joined my mother, sister, and children in the living room, seven in all. They were waiting on the couches for me to come and give them hope. As I walked through the door, they stopped talking and turned to me.

"Well, she died," I announced. They wept loudly, each of them, and their weeping caught me off guard. I wasn't part of the crying scene; it was taking place outside of me, and I was merely observing. Joy rose to hug me; then I sat on the floor and motioned for John Paul and Lauren to join me, one on each side, so I could put my arms around them.

John walked in with Dr. Anderson whom the whole family had come to know over the years. When my mother phoned him at the Methodist church that afternoon, he excused himself from choir rehearsal and came to be with us. He walked around greeting each of us and prayed, "Loving God, be with us in our great sorrow. . . ." He neither condemned Mary nor made her death sound as though, in light of faith, it wasn't all that bad.

He spoke of the power of baptism, bringing to mind how in 1978 most of us gathered there had celebrated Mary's baptism on an icy January day. Wearing a long white dress, she lay sleeping in my arms that day with love pouring forth all around her. We offered her to God in faith and later celebrated with champagne. I didn't comprehend the gravity of the sacrament. I didn't know she was being baptized into the death of the Lord as well as his life and resurrection. As Dr. Anderson spoke, I was offering Mary to God once again; I was frightened and my offer wavered.

FRONT: JOY, MOTHER, DADDY, AND MARJ. BACK: RITA, LAUREN, MARY AND KRISTINE, CHRISTMAS 1994.

On his way out Dr. Anderson told us that he would drop by the next day. As soon as the door closed, Tom said, "Okay, I'll go pick up some food. Any suggestions?" It was kind and normal sounding, as was my mother asking to set a plate of food on my lap.

But the kindness didn't stop me from saying, "Mary sucker punched me. She made me think she was better when, really, she had this all planned. She's humiliated me; it's like I'm hanging on a cross naked." Relatives put their heads down and went on eating.

"You and John had every right to be out of the house today," said my mother whose views carried an authority I couldn't disregard even as a teen. She closed her eyes and took a deep breath. "Losing a daughter . . . I can't imagine."

"Well, I have another." Robert Kennedy had said the same thing in 1963 when asked about losing his brother John: "Well, I have another." Sixteen years old at the time, I thought those words among the noblest I'd ever heard. I just never expected to use them the way Kennedy had used them. But some sort of encouragement needed to be delivered on the evening of Mary's death, and without a vocabulary of my own, I had to borrow. My mother looked at me, and her gray eyes cut through the bravado to the heartache. In her seventy-fifth year, she understood something about the death of a child that I was far from knowing.

Born in October after three brothers had died of dysentery during the summer of 1920, my mother would always say, "Imagine what Mama went through being pregnant with me. Imagine." But I couldn't imagine; and the time I asked about her sister Elizabeth dying on an operating table in 1930s rural Georgia she said, "That was the only time I ever saw Mama fall down on the floor in grief." My mother had spent her whole life weighing up the death of children, and until that day, I had spent no time.

Around 7:30 that night, men in black knocked on the door. Father Dave and our pastor, Father Joe, walked into our gathering and hugged everyone even before the introductions. After leading us in the Our Father, Father Joe sat in a chair next to me, and I took his hand. He exuded confidence like Robert De

Niro playing a movie priest, and that helped me believe everything would be all right. Just as the room got quiet, John said, "I'm very concerned about the soul of my daughter."

"Well," Father Dave said, "the church's teaching about suicide isn't as harsh as it used to be." That was all he said.

Father Joe remarked on the unpredictability of teen behavior. He said that some teens find suicide attractive when they can't see their way out of a problem. When I said, "*Won't* see a way out," he corrected me with, "*Can't* see a way."

As far as I was concerned, Mary's suicide was a monumental "won't see." I wasn't going to argue with my pastor, although from that day I was bound to suicide as neither of the good celibate men in my living room would ever be. Suicide was no longer an abstraction floating out on the edges of my life. My daughter was enmeshed in it, and it was part of me.

Father Dave had his head turned to John Paul sitting beside him. Suddenly, the expression on the priest's face changed from polite interest to alarm. He looked around the room as if to say, "Is anyone else hearing what I'm hearing?"

Moving over to where they were sitting, I heard John Paul say he felt out of control. He said he couldn't be sure what he might do while he was driving. He was smiling a little. The sensation within me was that of falling off a cliff as in a dream. *How did my family get to this hellish place?*

Taking Father Dave aside, I explained that John Paul was under psychiatric treatment and would be getting extra attention. I tried to reassure John Paul, too, but aside from keeping him out of his car, I didn't know how to protect him. At least for that moment, he was safe. That was all anyone had or would have for a long time: one trance-like moment after another in the presence of heartsick people, hoping.

When the room grew quiet I said, "This is something like 'sitting shivah,' isn't it? You know, the Jewish practice of sitting with the dead."

"Yep," Father Joe said, though he probably knew I had it wrong. Shivah is seven days of communal mourning that takes place after a Jewish funeral, not before, allowing mourners to sit together and bear their loss. But Mary was with us in the living room, and we were sitting with her. I felt her compassion. I felt she realized what she'd done and was profoundly sorry for it; and even though I'd been angry with her earlier, I now wanted to sit with her forever.

Before that September night, I had lived forty-eight years mostly untouched by death. No one with whom I shared daily life had ever died, so I'd had no practice in the grieving arts. I was thinking that if John, the kids, and I were to survive, we needed grief counseling. We needed to drop everything we might normally be doing on a weekday afternoon and sit in a room with a bereavement counselor. We needed to listen closely to each other. (But hadn't we always?) John and I needed to come to terms with the ways we failed Mary. (But what about the ways she failed us?) We all needed to figure out how to help ourselves and each other.

Father Joe wrote down the name of a grief counselor and handed it to me. Relieved that someone might consider working with us, I was also wary of psychological scrutiny at the worst moment of our lives. And to think that the person who'd be missing from the counseling room was the one who put the four of us there; that was just galling.

As everyone was getting up to leave, Joy shouted, "It's not fair!"

Father Joe didn't tell her life is unfair; he merely looked at her amiably. "You'll be amazed by the reaction," he said. "Her friends will overwhelm you. Brace yourselves." I was glad to hear it; I wanted to be amazed and overwhelmed.

Once our visitors had gone, I went upstairs to close Mary's bedroom door. I meant to close it against havoc: the unmade bed, the cluttered desk, the shoes and jumbled clothing, the stubborn questions, and, more than anything else, Mary's complete and utter absence. On a previous Sunday night, she would have been sitting on her bed in a bright corner chatting on the phone with her friend Kelli, but not this night. All that was left was a dark, disheveled place in which she had gone out from this life. *Gone out from this life.* I closed the door.

John Paul and Lauren followed me into our bedroom. They looked weary and frightened. "You're safe in your rooms," I said. "Nothing bad is going to happen."

"That's right," John said. "We're all here together. You can leave your doors open if you want to, and we'll keep the hall light on."

Lauren gave me a clinging hug, and I wanted to hold onto her forever. John and I wrapped our arms around John Paul. "You're okay for tonight, aren't you?" I asked. He said he was, and then he and Lauren went to their rooms.

After locking the front and back doors, John came upstairs and said, "I never thought the real danger was right here in the house."

"Who would have thought? She really put one over on us, didn't she?" Seeing a videocassette lying on the dresser, I swept it across the room with my hand, startling John.

"Come on, now," he said.

"Come on, what? Mary was watching that video last night in our bedroom when I went in and told her that you and I were planning to watch *A Man for All Seasons.* She switched off the video without comment, and as the screen turned blue I said that it looked like a movie theater in here. Mary then got up and walked out of the bedroom, and it was the last time I ever saw her. How dare she watch a video as though everything was fine when obviously it wasn't fine? That's what I want to know."

Around 11 p.m., only twenty-four hours after Mary had been eating ice cream, John and I pulled back the covers for bed. We held each other and wept, but there was no comfort and, in the end, nothing to say. After a few minutes, John's breathing grew deeper as he drifted off. Hearing no sound from John Paul or Lauren, I figured they'd also gone to sleep. In my imagination, I was climbing out of my body and blowing across a prairie, like tumbleweed. Not only could I not relax, but I believed I didn't deserve to relax. If I'd been more alert and less relaxed the night before, maybe Mary would still be alive.

An hour after John turned off the light, the phone rang. Earlier at the hospital, he had signed papers donating Mary's organs; and the organ-removal people from Georgetown University Hospital were on the phone wanting to know which organs they could remove.

"Skin? Yes," John said.

"Bone marrow? Okay."

"Eyes?"

"Wait a minute," I said. "How will they do that? What will it look like?"

John asked the caller and then said, "They'll place something in the sockets and sew the eyelids shut. It should look okay." Mary's eyes taken out and her sockets *filled* with something, for God's sake, so they'd look okay? But I agreed to it because someone somewhere could benefit, and someone needed to benefit.

After dozing a couple of hours, I woke before dawn, washed my hair, and dressed. Everyone else was still asleep, but on a normal Monday morning the house would have been coming to life. I would have heard Mary's routine before she left for school: showering and blowing her hair dry; closing the refrigerator door and plopping her cereal bowl on the kitchen table; slamming the back door, then the car door before starting the engine. On a normal Monday morning, I would have gone into her room and given her a hug good-bye; and smiling slightly, she would have returned my hug. As she left, I would have said a prayer for her.

On a normal Monday morning, John and I would have been propped in bed praying psalms from Ordinary Time during the Liturgy of the Hours. On this Monday morning, however, John and I were praying the Office for the Dead from our familiar red *Christian Prayer*. We could hardly have done otherwise, though even prayers for the dead begin with the rousing "Come, let us sing to the Lord and shout with joy to the Rock who saves us" from Psalm 95. We prayed haltingly. From Psalm 40: "I waited, I waited for the Lord and he stooped down to me; he heard my cry"; and from Psalm 42: "My tears have become my bread, by night, by day, as I hear it said all day long: 'Where is your God?'"[6]

We took turns reading the verses, and the rhythm calmed me. From Paul's first letter to the Corinthians, I started reading, "Tell me, if Christ is preached as raised from the dead, how is it that some of you say there is no resurrection of the dead? If there is no resurrection of the dead, Christ himself has not been raised. And if Christ has not been raised . . ."[7]

A moment earlier, I had thought no amount of prayer too much to offer for Mary, but it quickly got to be too much. "John,

I can't finish this. It's too wordy, and I don't have the energy." He put down his prayer book and began to dress.

At that instant, the beeping started. From behind Mary's door came an electronic beeping: her alarm clock. Why hadn't the stupid thing sounded on Sunday morning when it might have done some good? John said it must have been knocked and reset in the rescue commotion the day before. We hurried down the hall to turn off the clock but found the door still locked. John Paul joined us and shoved his shoulder into the door, dislodging a full-length mirror that had been attached to the back. The mirror crashed to the floor in a hundred shards, and John had to sidestep the broken glass to shut off the alarm.

"Unbelievable," he said. After standing in the gray light of her room for a minute, we stepped out and closed the door.

Upon arriving for early Mass, we spoke to no one but walked to the front pew and sat by ourselves. As long as I stared straight ahead, I could withstand the inner churning. The lector began with, "Let us pray for Mary Kathryn Antus who died yesterday," and Deacon Williams finished with, "Go in peace to love and serve the Lord." None of it was the least bit real.

Sister Maureen strode down the aisle toward us, her face filled with sorrow. As principal of our parish school, she'd heard the news from Father Joe. More than most people, she had seen Mary's potential, had written letters of recommendation for her, and presented academic awards to her. Now looking squarely at John and me, she said, "We want to help any way we can. When Lauren comes back to school, we'll take extra special care of her. You know that."

The truth is, I didn't know that. I didn't know until Sister Maureen was standing in front of me how she or anyone else in the parish would respond. But there they were, teachers and neighbors coming up to us in the aisle, asking what happened and looking shocked and sad.

On other Monday mornings in 1995, John would have left for the hospital after Mass to make patient rounds. I would have gotten Lauren off to school, gathered my textbooks, and headed for my Christology class at Washington Theological Union where I was studying for a master's degree in theology. On a normal autumn Monday in 1995, I would have felt anxious about the forty-mile commute but happy to arrive at the school and take my seat. On this abnormal morning, however, John and I found my sister in the kitchen plugging in a coffee urn when we got back from Mass. Joy had covered the dining room table with a good tablecloth and arranged flowers and white china coffee cups on it.

"How was your night?" she asked.

"I didn't sleep much, but the kids are still asleep. What about you?" I replied.

"I didn't sleep at all. But I plan to keep moving."

Joy was preparing for a social day. She knew mourners would be dropping by and was dressed nicely to greet them. She knew they would need coffee and some sort of little pastry. As always, she was helping me cross a threshold of new responsibility. On my wedding day as she buttoned up the sleeves of my dress, for instance, she told me that right before my vows I should hand my bouquet to her, but I didn't listen. When John Paul was born a couple years later, she came to the hospital and showed me how to support his wobbly head, and I did listen. On this first day without Mary, she was taking over the kitchen and all the hospitality because I was incapable of listening or much else. Someone had to set petite coffee cups over against the morning's bleakness, and it was naturally going to be her.

John and I sat down to breakfast, but I sensed that the corn flakes would sit like corn husks and ended up eating little. I kept seeing Mary's blue lips, and I couldn't stop visualizing the violence done to a body once so healthy and such an intimate part of mine. My face flushed at the thought of it.

The doorbell rang. On the front porch stood a husband and wife from All Saints Parish who had heard the announcement at the 8:30 Mass. Joy invited them in and asked if they wanted coffee. To my surprise, they accepted the offer. They were the first from our church to visit, and while I did not take their condolences for granted, I didn't see why they had to stay and drink coffee. John was on the phone, so I ended up sitting with them. I didn't want to tell them what I knew. Since when did I have to sit in my living room and discuss my daughter with coffee-sipping people? On the other hand, a young parishioner had died, and members of our church had a right to know something about it.

During those few moments, I became aware of the "bubble." As I later came to see, the bubble was a transparency between me and other people, a kind of membrane that muffled their voices and allowed me to act more or less evenly. I heard the wife say, "I am so sorry," and the husband say, "What a terrible, terrible thing." But the bubble provided me a place of inner calm from which I could reply, "Thank you. Yes, it *is* terrible." That was pure shock at work in me, of course, and had nothing to do with moral strength.

When Mary's high school chaplain phoned, I heard myself say from inside the bubble, "We believe in the resurrection," to each offered kindness.

"The faculty and staff here at Paul VI extend our deepest sympathy, Mrs. Antus," Father Mark said.

"Well, Father, we believe in the resurrection."

"The entire school community has been praying and will continue to pray for Mary and all of you."

"Thank you, Father. We do believe in the resurrection. We believe Mary is with God and she's praying for us. That's what we believe."

My mother arrived mid-morning with her head down, neatly attired, a living illustration of one of her favorite sayings: "You can get through anything by getting dressed in the morning and going to work." That's what she'd done every morning for three decades as office manager in Tom's business.

"Something awful happened a few minutes ago," she said. "I was looking at a picture of Mary on our refrigerator door, and your father saw me crying. He said, 'What's wrong?' When I told him our Mary was gone, he said, 'Who's Mary?'"

"Well, that must have been . . . he doesn't know anything?"

"No."

My father was seventy-nine years old and had Alzheimer's disease. For the past five years, he had been losing ground to the illness. That morning, my mother laid out for him a bright blue sweater that caught the azure of his eyes. She helped him get into the car to come be with us, and here they were. Daddy wandered through the living room with a glass of water.

"Hi," he said.

"Hi, Daddy." He frowned a little, apparently realizing something was off kilter about the morning, but I think that's all he realized. My father had been an electronics engineer who had once built television sets, cultivated peach trees, and extracted honey from beehives he had made. Now he was living in his own bubble. Until that morning, I never thought I could envy him in his state of permanent unknowing. He would never have to feel what I was feeling and, unlike me, he

33

was not plagued with questions. He was simply who he was: a white-haired gentleman standing in front of me with a glass of water, and I missed him.

By late morning, nine people were milling around the kitchen and dining room, all members of my family. No one spoke directly about Mary. When John Paul wandered in, my mother asked how he'd slept; Joy asked if he'd like scrambled eggs. My brother, George, said, "Johnny!" before hugging him.

John Paul said he'd slept all right, and while he looked ill at ease, I saw nothing unusual about the way he was acting. Of course, who was I to gauge a child's behavior? John Paul was vulnerable and needed someone like George with him throughout the day. Everyone knew that.

MARY, LAUREN, HUDSON, KRISTINE, AND JOHN PAUL IN BOSTON, SUMMER 1993.

John and I went upstairs to phone Dr. Matthews who was crying when she answered. John and she talked about increasing John Paul's medications and providing him a safe place to stay for a few days away from our noisy house. Then I heard John say, "No, we don't have any guns . . . and get all pain medications out of the house? Okay." *She's just being cautious. Who can blame her?* But it was crazy talk, just the same—a disruption of trust in the reliable person I thought John Paul to be. Getting everyone's attention that morning was his capacity for self-violence.

Not that I was overlooked. A neighbor showed up and shadowed me. When I went into the living room, Patricia followed, and when I walked down the hall, she came right behind. "Imagine losing a daughter this way!" I said.

She leaned in close but did not reply. With her background in clinical psychology she likely knew the signs of unhinged grief, and I think she was looking for them in me. It's true that I was desperate to be with Mary again, but I was also desperate to hold my family together. Apart from that, I was too muddle-headed to think about, much less carry off, any arrangement that included my actual death. I was already living a kind of death, and what I most needed was someone to listen without looking away.

Mary's best friend Kelli called and said, "Tell me it's not true. I stayed home from school today, but Sandra left school to come tell me. I just had to hear it from you."

"Well, I'm afraid . . ."

"But I just saw Mary in homeroom Friday. She seemed fine to me."

"We thought so too." That was all I could offer, but I knew Mary's friends needed more than that from me.

A little later, I got another opportunity. Lisa's mother called to say, "My daughter was a friend of Mary's. She's hysterical and won't listen to me. Would you please talk to her?"

"I'll try." I had to stand in for Mary and encourage her friends the way she herself would have done. I told Lisa how Mary had always liked her and how, I was certain, she had not meant to hurt her. I spoke well of my daughter; she deserved that much from me. At the same time, I was separating myself from what she had done.

"She spent a peaceful weekend here with us," I said. "There were no arguments. Nothing bad happened to make her do what she did."

Lisa took it quietly, and it seemed I was mothering both her and Mary at the same time.

The doorbell was soon ringing with neighbors dropping off ham, salad, rolls, and brownies. It brought to mind occasions when I had been offered gifts out of a depth of generosity that left me not knowing how to say thank-you; in this instance, not so much for the food but for people entering into my loss and easing the isolation. I had no idea anyone would choose to sit beside me at the kitchen table, but Linda did so. My friend put a big purple chrysanthemum on the table and surprised me by saying, yes, she'd like to have a ham sandwich with me.

Before long, a family celebration appeared to be taking place: homemade cakes and pies in the dining room, the arrival of flowers, relatives and acquaintances embracing and talking. I wouldn't have believed it possible, but there was even laughter. All the while, part of me was waiting for a phone call from Mary. I was expecting to pick up the phone and hear her sweet voice say, "Sorry I'm late, Mom. I'll be home in a while." Part of me was watching for her to come through the door to the applause of her grandparents, aunts, uncles, and cousins. It was what she'd done on birthdays and other happy occasions, and I was looking for it.

At the same time, part of me was asking, "Is Mary aware of what is taking place here today? Is there any chance she is experiencing something like it right now? Is this gathering a sign of hope for her?"

My mother suggested that John and I go upstairs and rest. I did want to rest but, once on the bed, realized how difficult it was going to be. All day, there had been a quotation careening through my mind that grew distinct in the quiet of the bedroom. It came from Daniel Patrick Moynihan who had served in the Kennedy administration. At the time of President Kennedy's funeral, columnist Mary McGrory had said to him, "We'll never laugh again."

Moynihan replied, "Mary, we'll laugh again. But we'll never be young again." McGrory was closer to the truth in my estimation; I couldn't see myself ever laughing again.

Lying on my side and looking at oak branches through the window soothed me, and I began thinking of the statue of Teresa of Avila in the Carmelite monastery chapel. It's a portrayal of the saint standing with a quill in one hand and a book in the other, gazing evenly ahead, not falling backward in ecstasy as she's sometimes shown. The statue speaks of her courage, which I now believed was available to me. Teresa said no words that I could hear, but her spirit was with me, saying, "Steady; you can survive this."

Both the phone and the doorbell were ringing downstairs, and someone was answering every bell. Feeling protected, I sat up in bed beside John, shut my eyes, and prayed. That's when a scene passed before my closed eyes showing three human figures emerging from a shadowy grotto on the left and walking to the center. With their backs to me, they bowed in unison to a horizon of bright, creamy light before disappearing.

My heart seemed to throb out of rhythm. Something unprecedented—a vision, I sensed—had appeared in front of my lowered eyelids. Backlit by the brilliant light, the profiles of those three people appeared only in silhouette. But I knew the figure on the right was Jesus, the one on the left was the Blessed Mother, and my daughter Mary was in the middle. It was clear to me that Jesus and his mother had taken care of my daughter and introduced her to God. I hadn't conjured the vision out of fatigue or emotion; I believe it had simply flowed into the core of my being as a sort of divine consolation. My response: *So this is supposed to make me feel better? Well, it doesn't.* But the vision stayed with me just the same, injecting a sort of calm into my chest cavity.

When I went down to the kitchen a couple of hours later, my mother was putting a sprig of brown leaves in a vase. "A neighbor wanted you to have this. He just came back from the Holy Land, and these are olive leaves from the Garden of Gethsemane."

As I fumbled with words of amazement, my mother placed the olive leaves on the windowsill where they sat throughout the week. I never found out who gave them to us.

Endnotes

5 1 John 4:12, *The New American Bible* (Wichita, Kansas: Catholic Bible Publishers, 1983), 1328.

6 Psalms 95:1; 40:2; 42:4, *Christian Prayer: The Liturgy of the Hours* (New York: Catholic Book Publishing Co., 1976), 688, 1474, 1477.

7 1 Corinthians 15:12-14, *Christian Prayer: The Liturgy of the Hours* (New York: Catholic Book Publishing Co., 1976), 1478.

3

LEAVE TAKING

We die with the dying:
See, they depart, and we go with them.
We are born with the dead:
See, they return, and bring us with them.
T. S. ELIOT[8]

WEDNESDAY OF MARY'S WAKE WAS warm with clear sunlight and deep shade, a heartbreaking day. Viewings were scheduled at Lee Funeral Home for afternoon and evening and, in preparation, I spent considerable time that morning thinking about what I should wear. Clothing was the one thing I could control. I thought mourners might be viewing me as well as Mary, and I wanted to show composure. It mattered that I look nice for my daughter because I still thought she might care how I looked, especially around her friends.

After lunch, I put on my black dress with tiny white accents, dark stockings, and black patent leather pumps. It was a way of putting on decorum and setting up margins on an excruciatingly public day. I went into Mary's room, found the gold love-knot earrings Joy and Tom had given her on her sixteenth birthday, now mine, and put them on.

The funeral director had asked John and me to come to the funeral home before the afternoon viewing to see whether Mary had been satisfactorily dressed and her makeup properly applied. "How could we be expected to do such a thing?" I wanted to know. But it was one of the rituals of letting go that had been coming at us from every direction. Three days had passed since I last saw Mary at the hospital, and I yearned for her face, her voice, her laugh; though seeing her laid out was something else again— a revolting prospect. I thought I was steeled to it until I started weeping in the car on the trip over just because I couldn't get an aspirin container open.

What I noticed first upon seeing Mary was her pleasant smile. It captured everything good about her. Then: *Oh, God, she's really dead.* Heading to the nearest chair, I sat down and cried. She was completely and permanently gone, and there was nothing I could do about it. John and his brother Robert sat silently in their gray suits and looked down at their hands. I went over to kneel at the prie-dieu by the casket. Finding no prayer words, I simply gazed at Mary's face. Pink light softened her features but did not hide the large bruise on her right cheek. What caused that blueness, and why? Why did she have to suffer?

JOHN WITH MARY AND LAUREN AT HILTON HEAD ISLAND, 1989.

LAUREN AND MARY AT HILTON HEAD ISLAND, 1989.

A few feet away stood a display of family pictures featuring Mary. There was one of her in my arms smiling up at me as I smiled down at her on the day of her baptism. Another showed her as a toddler playfully biting John's nose. In one, she clutches the car while standing in the driveway on roller blades; and in another she runs with her hair blowing in the wind on a Hilton Head beach.

The most compelling photograph was the one taken on our family vacation at Lake Placid five weeks earlier. It showed John with his arms around Mary and John Paul. Mary's hand was touching Lauren's elbow. Mary smiled in the slanting afternoon sunlight and tilted her head toward Lauren just before I took the picture. "Oh, that's going to be a nice one," I remembered saying. No one nearing the casket at the wake could possibly overlook those pictures; no one could walk away with a single, horrific impression of Mary or our family. That was our intention.

When my niece, Kristine, taped the final picture on the poster board the night before and held it up for me to see, I ran to my bedroom and sat on the floor weeping. Joy appeared beside me a moment later; and I said, "How am I supposed to live without her?"

"You have a son and a daughter who need you. That's how."

"I know that, but how am I supposed to live without *her*?"

Standing in the funeral parlor, I now wondered how I was supposed to live through the day of viewings. Joy, Lauren, and my mother walked into the funeral home foyer. Lauren was wearing the trim navy blue skirt and sweater she had gotten just the day before. She was pale and much too delicate for what she was about to do, and I wanted to walk her out the front door and away. Putting my arm around her, I said, "You don't have to do this if you don't want to, but we can go see Mary, just you and me."

"Okay." We entered the empty room and held Mary's cold hand.

"She's being warmed by God's love now." We knelt for a moment. As though sedated, Lauren neither commented nor cried. Years later, she told me the odor of embalming fluid had disgusted her that afternoon.

My mother came up to me in the hall and said, "John Paul has gone in, and he cried."

"Well, at least he's in touch with reality."

Over the past day or so, he had grown mistrustful of John and me and only reluctantly agreed to enter our house at all. Fortunately, our neighbor Patricia had said he could stay at her house down the street where it was quiet. I glimpsed him down the hall, somber and handsome in his new blazer, and worried that he might never trust us again. After seeing Mary, he left the funeral home with Patricia and did not return. Loving eyes would be watching him, I told myself; and I put John Paul out of my mind. I had to. People were filing into the viewing room several at a time.

That moment and the following hours brought forth good-will unlike any I had experienced. Words of consolation, genuine and heartfelt, were not what set the day apart. It was the willing-ness of people to stand alongside John and me that made the day exceptional. Flowing through the sizable room, down the hall, and out the front door hundreds of people stood, waiting to speak to us: Mary's friends and teachers, students in school uniforms, her old boyfriend, my old boyfriend, neighbors I saw frequently and those I saw rarely, doctors, nurses, parishioners, Lauren's friends, Carmelites, priests from Mary's high school, professors from my school, Benedictine sisters along with our own sisters, brothers, aunts, uncles, and cousins.

Seeing was not believing. Seeing Mary in the casket was not a matter of believing she was dead and thinking, "Now I understand," but rather the opposite: "How could this possibly have happened? Why would Mary do such a thing?" I wasn't expecting to give or receive answers that day. Whenever someone asked me a question about Mary, I usually said, "I don't know." But I did want to find out what I could from those who had been with her on her last day of school.

Classes had been in session only three weeks, but Mary's new teachers all came to the viewing. What could they tell me about a student they barely knew? Grasping my hand one man said, "I was Mary's government teacher. Something I don't understand—she handed in a paper just last Thursday."

"It doesn't make any sense, does it?" I said, as though allied with a government teacher against my daughter. "Why would she be doing school work?"

"For the life of me, I don't know," he said before shrugging and stepping aside.

I wondered whether Mary was hopeful until the day she died or whether she was acting normal to keep from alerting her teachers. How was I ever going to know?

"When I lectured," said a young teacher of women's literature, "I lectured with your daughter in mind, Mrs. Antus. She always seemed to know what I was getting at."

When she said "your daughter," the woman raised both arms and dropped them down in front of me as though to emphasize "your daughter and no one else's daughter." The comment didn't surprise me; Mary had been wise all her life. When she was six or seven years old, I occasionally read aloud letters from the Ann Landers advice column to see what Mary herself would advise. It was fun because she took it seriously and sometimes gave sound advice. Another question thus formed as I talked to the literature teacher: *If Mary was so discerning about people's ways, how could she have been so disastrously wrong about her own life?*

During the four hours of viewing, dozens of Mary's school friends waited in line to speak with John and me. This is what I found out from them: she didn't talk much to her friends at lunch that last Friday. Otherwise, everything she did was the thing she always did; her behavior aroused no suspicions. What affected me most in those teens, though, was not what they knew or didn't know about Mary. It was their raw sadness.

One young woman began screaming beside the casket, and though John took her aside and tried to calm her, she was still crying as friends led her away. Was she thinking of suicide herself? Were any of them thinking of suicide? Most looked angry and flustered, but after telling me their names they usually smiled a little and said something like, "I sat right beside her in French class. It's not going to be the same without Mary." Behind their beautiful young faces, what was really going on?

"I'm sorry Kelli, Debbie, Michelle, and every other teen in this room. I'm sorry for what my daughter has done to you. Thank you for coming; you were a good friend. Mary always thought you were funny, interesting, smart . . . I know she'd want me to tell you that." Debbie handed me a poster full of pictures of Mary with farewell messages scrawled underneath. When I saw "I'll always remember your beautiful voice," I was overcome and handed the poster to someone else.

After talking with John and me early in the evening, one teen went to the back of the line and waited for another turn. "Why, Andrew," John said, "didn't we just see you awhile ago?"

"Yes," he said. Andrew and his friends were needy, but unlike Mary, they were open about it. She had lost faith in John and me—who could deny it?—but her friends were looking to us for comfort, and I wanted to comfort them.

Mary's former boyfriend, Tim, approached. They had broken up in April and I hadn't seen him since, though I'd seen pictures of him, the lighthearted ones Mary left on the bedroom floor next to her suicide note, a gesture I hadn't even tried to figure out. Wearing a white shirt and tie, Tim smiled shyly; but when John embraced him, the young man's back straightened and his arms remained down.

Looking into his eyes I said, "We don't think this was anyone's fault, Tim. Mary was sick." It was all I could manage; I hoped it was enough. Tim flashed the radiant smile my daughter had found so enchanting and moved on.

I was now all by myself receiving people and growing thirsty with no way of moving to the left or right or asking for a drink of water. John had decided to shorten everyone's wait by working his way down the line and saying hello so they could go home, but they hadn't gone home. They'd stayed to speak to me and ended up standing close and holding my hand. It was intimate, and I couldn't turn away.

With Dr. Roberts, who delivered Mary, and Dr. Montano, the pediatrician who held her within an hour of her birth—with all John's doctor friends—I relied on the standard medical explanation: "Mary was sick" or "Our daughter was receiving psychiatric treatment for depression. It was much worse than we knew, obviously." I instructed one general practitioner on the slipperiness of the illness as though he hadn't heard about it: "Depression is a wicked illness. It's not like a rash you can see or a fever you can measure. We honestly thought she was getting better, but when you think they're getting better can be the most dangerous time. That's what I've heard anyway."

"You're absolutely right," Dr. DeGrassi said, and though it was nice to be right about something, John and I were wrong about the one thing that mattered: keeping our daughter safe. Calling Mary sick came closest to framing her suicide in a non-judgmental way, but it continued to raise a question about John and me: how was it possible that while Mary slept under our roof and ate at our table we did not know how sick she really was?

It was a day of conundrum, but most people shied away from questions. Only Larry from our church drew himself up in front of me and said, "Why?" When I didn't answer, he moved away. Next in line stood Kathy who had wallpapered Mary's bedroom some years before and chatted with me about that ordinary wallpapering day as though it had been the best day of our lives. It had been the best day, or one of them. A best day was now any day which included Mary.

My daughter and Sarah, a neighborhood friend, had taken weekend trips to the Blue Ridge Mountains. When Sarah's father approached, he touched my arm without stopping and said, "There are no words." I turned to watch him walk away: *Dave is right.*

Even Meg had no words that day, and Meg always had words. As the director of a pro-life center in Manassas, Virginia, she could think on her feet better than anyone I'd ever seen. When I'd volunteered at the pro-life center, I'd heard her counsel pregnant women in a variety of hopeful ways. No matter what reason they gave for choosing to terminate their pregnancies, Meg always came up with life-giving words and backed up the words with groceries, baby clothes, and rent payments.

When all Meg could say to me was, "Ah . . . ," I realized all over again how bad things were and cried along with her. But tears were better than having to pretend.

"God is good," said one smiling Benedictine sister; "God is good."

"Yes, Sister, God is good."

"Your daughter is in a better place," many said. *What was the matter with this place? And what better place is she supposed to have gone to, and how could she have gone there ahead of me?* An older lady said I had an angel watching over me. *People can't be angels. Don't you understand? What I hope for is a saint.*

And early the next morning while jogging around the neighborhood, I kept seeing an image of Mary. Her smiling face was in the black sky above and on the black street below. Maybe she hadn't really left me after all. Maybe she was finally peaceful; maybe she was blissful. When I returned to the house, I phoned my mother who was scheduling a home caretaker to stay with my father during the funeral. Her hello was husky with sorrow, but I thought I could lift her spirits a little. "I think Mary is happier now. Maybe she'll be able to help each of us the way we most need."

"Well, I hope so," she said. "Mary is my heart."

Mary and her Grandmother Joyce, 1979.

49

Mary had spent winter Saturdays at my parents' house years before when my father was growing cranky and forgetful with Alzheimer's. Just seeing her granddaughter pull shoes and dresses out of the closet and try them on had made my mother happy. At a Christmas dinner in 1993, my mother had stood before fifteen of us in her family room and given a little talk about what we'd all meant to her.

When it came to Mary, she said, "What good times we've had together with you coming over and playing dress-up with scarves, boots, old jewelry, and anything else you could find in my dresser drawer. I also like the advice you gave granddaddy when you were just a little tot. You told him, 'You've got a lot to learn about grandma. You gotta be more patient with her.' Smart kid!"

During my phone conversation with my mother before the funeral, I realized nothing was going to make her happy that morning or for a thousand mornings to come, so what I wanted to ask my daughter was this: "Before swallowing the pills, did you stop for one second to think of your grandmother? And if not, why not?"

Mr. Marshall called around eight that morning. He was the handyman who'd helped us around the house for years, and there was no job he wouldn't tackle. One day I came home from the grocery store to find Mary and Mr. Marshall cutting old carpet from her bedroom floor and heaving the bundles out the second-floor window. They seemed to be enjoying it.

That was then. Now Mr. Marshall was on the phone wanting to talk about dirt. "Mrs. Antus, can I come over today and bring a load of topsoil for that low place in the front yard?" *Topsoil; front yard.* The words were far too normal. They brought to mind ordinary mornings of an ordinary life now lost to me, and I didn't think I would ever care about my front yard again.

Mary had left this earth, and part of me had gone with her and was not coming back.

"Mr. Marshall, I'm sorry to tell you this." I broke it to him in three pieces: first the death, then the cause, and then the reason: depression. I told him the funeral would begin in a couple of hours and that I would like him to come if he could, but he abruptly ended the conversation. I heard him cry out before the connection was broken.

The funeral was scheduled for ten o'clock at All Saints Church. I looked forward to it. I looked forward to going home with Mary one last time to a church that had been central to the life of my family. It was the pastor of All Saints who stretched the rules, I always thought, by agreeing to marry John and me in 1972 when I wasn't Catholic and John wasn't a member of the parish. And it was an announcement in the All Saints bulletin in 1977 that put me on a good path. It said that an inquiry class for those interested in learning about the Catholic faith would begin in September and could lead, if one chose, to joining the Catholic Church.

That summer, John Paul was three years old and Catholic; and I was seven months pregnant with Mary who likewise would be baptized Catholic. Looking down at my round belly I kept thinking, "This baby is going to be Catholic, and I'm not." Unsettling as it was, that dash of reality was urging me to something more than onlooker status at Sunday Mass, and I knew it. But there had also been a night when I saw John sitting on the edge of the bed praying for a patient that a single, crystallized desire floated to mind: *Whatever he has, I want.*

So I signed up for the inquiry class with the understanding that unless I heard something I couldn't live with, I was going to convert to Catholicism. A few months after Mary was baptized, I stood at the altar during the Easter Vigil Mass with John's hand on my shoulder, finally a Catholic like my husband and children. It was a moment of contentment greater than I had imagined, and it grew into years of contentment.

Lauren, John, Marj, Mary and John Paul outside All Saints Church, 1988.

Without knowing it, I'd entered into one of the most "ingenious communities that human skill has ever created," according to sociologist Andrew Greeley in describing the American Catholic parish. Greeley writes of the "overlapping relationship patterns" existing within neighborhood parishes that create energy or "social capital."[9] On the day of Mary's funeral, I was drawing on that capital. I was relying on the people of All Saints to ground me and give me strength.

Family members gathered at our house before the funeral on that warm, bright morning. I heard Joy talking with John's brother Paul and his wife Linda on the patio below our open bedroom window. My sister was arranging flowers in vases for the luncheon at All Saints, which was to follow the graveside service. Judging by their polite tones, it could have been the morning of a graduation or wedding. As John and I were dressing, though, he said he was worried about Mary's salvation. That alarmed me.

"You need to get over that 1950s theology of yours," I said. "It isn't helping."

"It's *not* 1950s theology," he said. "No one will let me talk about Mary's soul—not even my own wife!"

"Not here and not now, that's for sure."

I, too, was fearful for Mary but lacked energy for arguing. It was all I could do to dress and get to the church. Besides, nothing had taken place among the people we encountered that week which pointed to anything but God's goodness. It was a goodness which had permeated my life that I had not properly valued or even recognized. Now that I was desperate for it, I saw it almost everywhere.

A moment later in a kitchen full of flowers, I pulled two long-stemmed red roses out of a vase and handed one to Lauren so we could hold them during the funeral and leave them on the casket at the end.

When we arrived at All Saints, the clergy were waiting for us outside the church doors. The pallbearers, each an uncle or cousin to Mary, slid the casket from the hearse and wheeled it into the church foyer. Father Joe sprinkled it with holy water and then asked John and me to place the white linen pall over it. Down the entire length of the pall was sewn a purple cross, which John and I centered so the cloth would hang evenly over the casket. Father Joe handed John Paul a wooden cross and Lauren a Bible to place on top of the casket.

Then we started to move with the casket down the center aisle toward the altar, all eighteen family members. Ahead, an altar server swung the censer of pale aromatic smoke that rose through sunlight to the vaulted ceiling. As our family walked past rows of standing people, I kept my head low so I wouldn't see anyone or ever associate a parishioner's face with Mary's funeral.

When the casket reached the front of the church, the pallbearers situated it underneath the large Easter candle in front of the altar, which was surrounded by lilies and yellow chrysanthemums. It was exactly where Mary had received First Communion and not far from where she had been baptized. We entered the first pew where my family had sat dozens, if not scores, of times. I was moved to see so many clergy as they processed to the sanctuary: the three clerics from our parish along with three Oblates of St. Francis de Sales from Mary's high school and a brown-robed Brother Bryan from the Carmelite monastery in Washington. For an instant, they filled up a cavern of loss within me.

I was counting on the ritual of the Mass to speak of resurrection as thousands of words had failed to do, but I also wanted Father Joe to praise Mary and make all the questions about her float away on the incense. "Come to me, all you who are weary and find life burdensome, and I will refresh you," Father Joe read from Matthew's gospel. "Take my yoke upon your shoulders and learn from me, for I am gentle and humble of heart. Your souls will find rest, for my yoke is easy and my burden light."[10] Such a comforting beginning, but inasmuch as Mary was gone and could not be brought back, how was my burden ever to be made light?

The congregation grew still as Father Joe paused before beginning the homily. He seemed steady enough, but I felt sorry for him. Even with years of experience, what final word could he possibly provide?

"Sympathy sees and says, 'I'm sorry.' Compassion feels and whispers, 'I'll help.' Mary is a homily all her own. She is really

God's homily to us and has been throughout her life. She lived simply. She was quiet; she was beautiful; she was intelligent and talented." *Please don't stop. Say she was witty and gentle. Say she had a spirit unlike anyone else.*

"Her life is a gift of God that we shared in for too short a time," Father Joe continued. He said that Mary was created as God's daughter, that she was made in God's image and likeness and baptized into Christ's death. "His life, and suffering, his untimely death and resurrection give the hope that we, too, will live in the presence of the Lord forever if we so choose." I looked over at John. Did this language reassure him in any way? He seemed to be listening intently, but I couldn't tell.

At some point during the past few days, John had mentioned to Father Joe his discovery of Michael Quoist's book, titled *Prayers*, on Mary's bedside table. In the book was a slip of paper, marking "To Love: The Prayer of the Adolescent," which begins "I want to love Lord, / I need to love. / All my being is desire . . ." [11]

Father Joe told the congregation about John's discovery of this book and added, thoughtfully, that it was John and I who'd made it available to her.

I held Lauren's hand, and my mother patted me on the back; and out of the corner of my eye, I saw rows of uniform yellow shirts worn by students at Paul VI High School. Father Joe turned to the students. "For you young people gathered in such great numbers, Mary's death probably raises questions, one of which is, what are you going to do about it? After the pain and shock, after the anger and guilt, after the hurt and tears, what are you going to do with your lives in Mary's memory? If there is a fitting response to your friend's death, it is life—your life—a life that is lived better, more selflessly, honestly, and decently. Across the chasm of death, you can make Mary live."

He said Mary was heading for the eternal shore, that Jesus, who understands the human heart even when it goes wrong, would be waiting for her. He thanked God for her life with us and then concluded, "Farewell, Mary. Go forth in God's name. Be at peace."

MARY WITH FR. FAYAD ON THE MORNING OF HER FIRST COMMUNION, MAY 1985.

Wait! How can you be saying farewell? How could anyone be saying farewell to Mary? My pastor was leading me where I didn't want to go but, unlike me, he wouldn't have to stay there.

Once he'd finished his duties at the cemetery, he could go on with life as usual, it seemed to me, while I could not. After my restrained behavior throughout the morning, I felt like standing up and rending my garments. There ought to have been a rending and tearing. In the middle of the candles and pretty flowers, in the middle of a liturgy free of lamentation, I should have been allowed a little honest violence, if only to the clothes I was wearing. As it was, I put my head down and sat as still as possible.

Some months before, Father Dave had visited the Irish crystal store Kristine owned in Middleburg, Virginia, and remarked on the loveliness of a crystal altar set sparkling in the window. Because of his admiration for the altar set, my mother and sister donated it to All Saints Parish in Mary's memory. After Father Joe explained to the gathering that the chalice and paten would be engraved with Mary's name, Kristine and Joy brought the chalice, ciborium, paten, and cruets to the altar for blessing. As the chalice of ruby wine was elevated and placed in the middle of the altar, it threw off sparks of sunlight, an exquisite fusion of death and love. In that moment, I believed that the Eucharist, Christ's Body and Blood, would make Mary present to me and me to her. At communion, Father Joe surprised me by walking to the front pew where my family knelt and whispered, "The body of Christ." When he placed the wafer on my palm I could only say, "Thank you."

On the sidewalk after Mass, I caught up with Dr. Matthews who was heading to her car. She said, "That was quite a sermon. I was certainly challenged by what he said."

"So was I. For some reason, I feel peaceful right now; and I haven't been taking tranquilizers." Dr. Matthews smiled.

"By the way, John Paul is managing pretty well this morning," I added. "He's not going to the cemetery with us; he's going back to a neighbor's house where it's quiet." *See, despite the hearse and the casket and whatever you might think about me, I'm not shirking my responsibilities to John Paul or anyone else in the whole wide world.*

It was quiet in the car on the way to the cemetery. Lauren and I ate pears and drank water in the back seat. But I kept my eye on Mary up ahead in the black Cadillac hearse making her final pass through Civil War battlefields to a grave in Stonewall Memory Gardens. The hearse suddenly came up behind a tractor bumping along the country lane. "We're being led by a tractor," Tom said to John, with the slightest of smiles. I knew Mary would have laughed at the silliness of that, and I imagined her as lively and free.

Upon arrival at the cemetery, Lauren, John, and I walked to the canopy where blue chairs sat on plastic grass that ran up to the red clay hole over which the casket was suspended. Father Joe intoned his last few prayers, sprinkled the casket with holy water, and then gave each of us a prolonged embrace. When he finished, I motioned for Lauren to stand so we could both place our roses on the casket. We did so with our hands resting for an instant on the hard surface. After that, the pall bearers removed their delicate boutonnieres and laid them on the casket with the roses; and it was over. Lauren and I began making our way back to the car in the midday sun. I focused on my black patent leather shoes ticking through the grass as we walked away from Mary.

Endnotes

8 T. S. Eliot, "Little Gidding," *T. S. Eliot Collected Poems* (Franklin Center, PA: The Franklin Library, 1976), 201.

9 Andrew Greeley, *The Catholic Myth* (New York: Touchstone, 1990), 54-5.

10 Matthew 11:28-30, *Lectionary for Mass* (New York: Catholic Book Publishing Co., 1970), 977.

11 Michel Quoist, *Prayers* (New York: Avon Books, 1975), 52.

4

LIVING ON

A sacrament is physical, and within it is God's love; as a sandwich is
physical . . .
and within it is love, if someone makes it for you and gives it to you
with love; even harried or tired or impatient love . . .
ANDRE DUBUS[12]

GRIEF WAS NOT WHAT I thought it would be, at least not in the beginning. I expected drama and got something homespun. After the cemetery prayers, after lunch with fifty people in the All Saints school gymnasium, after solemn good-byes to out-of-town family, my brother, George, and I took our mother home. John and George's wife, Rita, came with us. When we arrived at the house, my father was sitting on the couch wearing khaki trousers and a sport shirt, his fine white hair neatly combed, his reading glasses sitting on the tip of his nose. Though he could no longer comprehend the words in front of him, he was holding up a section of *The Washington Post* as he'd done every day for thirty years.

"Howdy," he said as we walked up the foyer stairs.

The house was stuffy and smelled like saltines. "Don't you think we should open a window?" I asked my mother, and she agreed that we should. So I unhooked the latch and opened a window in my parents' house on a mild afternoon, their fifty-seventh wedding anniversary, though no one remarked upon the occasion. With nothing left to say, we sat down in our dark dresses and pearl earrings, our charcoal suits, Italian loafers and gold cufflinks. "After great pain, a formal feeling comes," Emily Dickinson wrote. "The Nerves sit ceremonious, like Tombs . . ."[13]

Linda walked in from a back room carrying a brush and hair rollers. For months, she had been staying with my father during the day while my mother worked. "Whew, you're back early. I was in the bedroom trying to tame this hair of mine." Motioning to my father, she added, "You had a good day, didn't you, George?"

My father pulled the newspaper down level with his eyes and said, "Hmm."

I've just left my daughter in a casket ten miles from here. My father does not know this and will never know it. Was Linda picking up on the dejection of five people sitting around all dressed up on a Thursday afternoon? Her pleasantries gave no hint of it, adding to the unreality.

When John and I got back to our house, I changed clothes and drove to the 7-Eleven to buy the latest *Manassas Journal Messenger* so that if anyone wanted to read Mary's obituary, we would have it. Scanning the notice, I saw that the date of death was accurate and that everyone's name was spelled correctly. I didn't like it that Mary was called "Antus," but at least the cause of death was omitted. If the word "suicide" had appeared, though, I'd already decided not to care. A few black squiggles on newsprint had no power over me. My eyes were now open to the reality that, apart from myself, I couldn't control anyone. I hadn't been able to control Mary, and I couldn't control what anyone thought or said about her death. It was liberating.

Something else was surfacing in the form of a lesson: Teresa of Avila taught her nuns to focus on pleasing God and to pay no heed to the opinions of others, favorable or unfavorable. She taught that a person's truest self is centered inwardly in God, not outwardly in opinion. Obituary in hand, it occurred to me how thoroughly I'd ignored that wisdom, having spent a good part of my life trying to figure out why people do what they do and then forming judgments around my speculations. But if I hadn't known what was taking place in my daughter's heart, how could I possibly know what is taking place in anyone else's? And even if I could know, might it not be charitable to ratchet down my opinions?

Late in the afternoon, John's brother Robert came over to the house from the Olde Towne Inn in Manassas where he was staying. He and I sat at the dining room table, which was full of flowers and sympathy cards, and had a beer. Robert had taught high-school English in Cicero, Illinois, for more than twenty years and had a storyteller's personality, which made him fun to be with. As we were talking about the day's events, one of Mary's friends knocked on the door and asked to see the display of family photographs that had gone from the wake to the funeral and was now sitting on the floor in the family room.

"Stay as long as you like, Kathy," I told her before going back to the dining room.

Robert looked up at me. "It's impressive how you've handled all this," he said.

"You would've done the same."

"I don't think so."

"Of course, it did get tedious having to repeat myself so much. If only I'd had a button that flashed, 'Thank you for your kindness,' and one that said, 'We're completely at a loss, too.'" We started laughing wildly. Kathy could hear us, and I regretted that a little but not enough to stop laughing.

She joined us in the dining room. "Do you think she suffered?"

I hated the question. *She suffered, all right. She suffered in this room and everywhere else. We just didn't see it.*

"Her father thinks she went into a coma pretty quickly," I said. "We don't think she felt anything."

That seemed to satisfy Kathy. It was a medical judgment John had voiced more than once. But who knew what took place with Mary as she lay dying? I couldn't bear to think about it for more than a second. I did know she sat with us at the kitchen table as a child asking the Blessed Mother to "pray for us sinners now and at the hour of our death."

At the luncheon hours earlier that day, I had taken comfort in the words of a friend. "I was imagining your daughter in the lap of the Blessed Mother during the funeral," she'd said. I thought she was probably talking about Michelangelo's Pieta on the back wall of our church behind the altar, a sculpture I'd studied many times over the years: the Virgin's wide shoulders and outsized lap, the deep folds of her garment, her sad serenity.

In the early days of John Paul's illness in 1992, that particular Pieta had broken through to me in a new manner. It had to do with the placement of the Virgin's hands. I'd noticed one morning that her right hand was supporting the weight of Jesus' lifeless body while her left was rising, palm up, in surrender.

When nothing was making sense in my world that year, when pep talks and reason were failing, those hands revealed a way forward with my dangerously sick son: support him with love; surrender him to God.

But on the night John Paul had been admitted to the psychiatric unit of Miami South Hospital in 1994, the psychiatrist told me, "Don't be anxious," when she heard my long sigh. Not only was I anxious, but I was also pessimistic. John Paul was ill, alone, and far away. His health was in jeopardy as was his enrollment at the University of Miami. It happened to be the day before Mary's seventeenth birthday, and we didn't know whether to celebrate her birthday, stay near the phone, or get on a plane for Miami.

"Look, Love, we're going to be upset about this," John had said, "but our son is safe and he's receiving good care. He's a thousand miles away, so there's not much we can do right now except pray. Why don't we go to Mass at the Shrine tomorrow? Then we can take Mary out to lunch in Georgetown."

That's how we came to be standing at the Mother of Sorrows chapel in the Basilica of the Immaculate Conception in Washington, D.C., on Mary's seventeenth birthday. Bronze reliefs on marble walls showed us the Blessed Mother's seven earthly sorrows. I wondered if, when Simeon told her a sword would pierce her heart, she felt the kind of anxiety I was feeling that morning and whether, meeting her son on his way to Golgotha, she was filled with pessimism. An argument could be made for it.

In their Sunday skirts and sweaters, Lauren and Mary bowed their heads and prayed the chapel prayer with us: "May she, who is our spiritual Mother and Patroness in heaven help us to find renewed strength at the cross of Christ." Standing alongside them, I couldn't help noticing the difference between this Mother of Sorrows and the Pieta at All Saints. The arms of this Mother were locked beneath and straining under the weight of Jesus' body while her head tilted back and her chin thrust forward in anguish. This Mother seemed to be bearing a thousand times my burden.

As the girls walked around the Pieta taking in the moment, I saw Mary look upward to the Virgin's face. It was a gaze I was now calling upon in my grief for her, the instant in which my daughter witnessed the grief of the Mother of Sorrows. On the day of Mary's funeral, my memory of that gaze gave hope that the Mother of Sorrows had, in turn, always and everywhere been looking with love upon my daughter.

So when Mary's friend Kathy walked into the dining room and asked, "Do you think she suffered?" I hadn't answered definitely. I did think any physical suffering Mary might have endured was over. Her illness was at an end, and she was free of it. I found a rough kind of peace in that.

Instead, what was circulating in my mind in the hours after the funeral was John Paul's distress. He was still staying in our neighbor Patricia's spare bedroom and refusing to come home. It was a jarring state of affairs that neither John nor I knew how to manage. But on Saturday evening, two days after the funeral, John said, "When we finish dinner, we should walk down to Patricia's and bring John Paul home. She can't be expected to keep him forever. Besides, he needs to be here with us."

"Right, he has to come home whether he wants to or not."

It made sense for us to walk John Paul home, but just because it made sense didn't mean it would happen. Life arrangements that formerly made sense—family togetherness, family safety—had been turned upside down, and it was alarming.

Ever since the funeral, John Paul had stayed clear of John and me. Who knew how he would act when we arrived at Patricia's? He was a big, muscular twenty-one-year-old who couldn't be made to do anything he didn't want to do, and we all knew it. Looking into the autumn twilight as we ambled toward our neighbor's house, I recited a verse of W. H. Auden's "Funeral Blues" that I'd been memorizing:

> The stars are not wanted now: put out every one;
> Pack up the moon and dismantle the sun;
> Pour away the ocean and sweep up the wood;
> For nothing now can ever come to any good.[14]

"Where are you getting *that?*" John asked. We were walking down the same Beauregard Avenue we had strolled many evenings before, but nothing about it was friendly. What I felt in the air was the opposite of friendly, some combination of dread and strangeness I had never experienced so intensely. It had been foolish to count on life's goodness lasting forever and naive to think love keeps children from all harm. And just how was I to offer emotional support to someone who didn't want to be around me anymore?

But then came the front-porch surprise: John Paul agreed to walk home with us. After mild protest, he gathered his things, thanked Patricia, and walked home across the grass. Loping upstairs, he went straight to the hall bathroom where he turned on the light, the fan, the ceiling heater, and sobbed behind the door.

"I don't know if we're going to make it," I said. The center was not holding and it seemed our family was going to pieces. John Paul needed nurturing that we couldn't possibly provide, and it was unrealistic for anyone to think we could provide it, given what we'd been through. "Maybe we should just go ahead and commit him."

"We can't have that kind of talk," John said. "At least he's here, and crying isn't the worst thing. It's probably the best thing."

John Paul calmed down after a few minutes and went to bed, as we all did. However precariously, we were together again in our home.

When the four of us went to Sunday Mass the next day, we sat in our usual front pew. John and I felt we had to keep *trying* and, to our relief, John Paul and Lauren were going along with it. They probably thought they had no choice, but they did have a choice. They could have refused or rebelled. That they chose to be with John and me returned a little of the family integrity Mary had taken.

Her suicide raised questions, at least in my mind, about how John and I were operating as parents and whether the inner workings of our family were predisposing our children to mental illness. Whether those questions would ever be answered and whatever the answers might be, John and I knew a good thing when we saw it. Going to Mass as a family was a good thing, as was everything else we did together; and we were not about to give it up.

At communion, I couldn't keep back tears when Father Jack placed the Eucharist in my hand. Colleen, sitting directly behind us, wept into her handkerchief, and I sensed that dozens of people throughout the church were praying for us by name. Just the same, when glowing pregnant women and their husbands came forward after Mass for a special blessing, it was not warmth I was feeling but bitterness: *You're going to have your hearts broken too. You just don't know it yet.*

In the interest of trying to do the right thing, we went out to lunch after Mass just as we'd done for years. It was a coming-out for our family, a first encounter with the world that knew nothing of our loss or the soundtrack in my head that kept repeating, "She is dead." Getting a table for four was easier than getting one for five. I noticed it immediately. Apart from that benefit, lunch was wretched in ways that had nothing to do with the food. While sitting at a table lit by sunbeams, we had few words for each other. I looked up at the drooping heads around the table and wondered if others in the restaurant could tell something was definitely not right with us. But other people were paying no attention. They chatted and laughed, heightening my loneliness.

John had visited Mary's grave the day before and suggested we all drive out to Stonewall Memory Gardens, which was a few miles from the restaurant. "We really ought to pay a visit to Mary," he said. "It's just something we ought to do." No one disagreed, so we rode in silence through green battlefields to the place where Mary lay. It was not a warm day, but heat radiated up my neck as we got out of the car.

"Without a grave marker," I said, "how will we know which one is hers?"

"Oh, I think you'll know." I didn't understand what John meant until we walked over to the plot. There, Mary was: six feet down inside a pile of dry, orange dirt covered with the up-ended containers of funeral flowers. Red snapdragons and lavender mums, purple orchids and white lilies—all flattened to the earth. *Honest to God, what a waste. Why would anyone throw these beautiful flowers in the dirt?*

Dropping to my knees, I bent over the soil and wept as everyone else stood silently. Mary should have been there with us in person, not in some horrible casket; it was impossible she was down in that sink of clay. The sun warmed my back as I continued kneeling over what I thought was the head of the grave. When John told me I was kneeling over Mary's feet, I realized how much I had to learn about cemetery custom and how disinclined I was to learn it.

"We forgive you, Mary," John said. *How can you be saying such a thing? Oh, I guess you're trying to set an example for the rest of us.*

That afternoon, Father Dave came to bless Mary's room. A friend had suggested it several days before, and I understood the implication: the room had been defiled and needed to be restored before God. We had to go back in there and pray in order to honor Mary and reclaim the room for our own. When Father Dave arrived with his book of blessings and bottle of holy water, we went up to Mary's room where, days before, my niece Kristine had picked up the shattered mirror pieces and dirty clothes, vacuumed the rug, and stripped and made the bed. Its navy blue bedspread was now dotted with red rose petals scattered by Lauren.

To the eye, it was a pleasant room. On a hot August day thirteen months before, Mary and I had begun a good-sized redecoration by steaming off the butterfly wallpaper. After we spent a couple of sweaty days together scraping paper globs, she painted the walls pale blue and the woodwork cream. She and Mr. Marshall later ripped out the green shag carpet to reveal light hardwood from which we pulled carpet tacks. Together we applied pine-scented paste wax and buffed the wood. "This is such an improvement," I said.

"It looks a whole lot better," she replied with satisfaction.

My biggest satisfaction had been working alongside her and seeing a part of her life I wouldn't ordinarily have seen. There was the moment, for example, when Mary said her boyfriend, Tim, might be moving from Manassas before the summer was out. The tears in her eyes sent a wave of pain through me. But what I've never forgotten was the smudge of blue paint on her cheek that made her look young and vulnerable.

John and I, along with John Paul and Lauren, now stood in the middle of Mary's room with our hands folded, waiting for Father Dave to begin the blessing. Mary could not have been more present or more absent.

"There used to be a crucifix on that wall," John said, with some embarrassment. "I don't know what happened to it."

"We painted this room last summer," I said. "I guess the crucifix just never got put back up."

"Well," Father Dave said, "I'm blessing not just the room but the family standing here." Raising his arms over us he asked that God "shower blessings on this family gathered here in your name. Enable those who are joined by one love to support one another. . . ." At the conclusion he prayed, "May the Lord Jesus, who lived with his holy family in Nazareth, dwell also with your family, keep it from all evil, and make all of you one in heart and mind."[15]

He then sprinkled holy water around the room. It was the most comforting moment of the day and, wanting to make it last, I invited Father Dave downstairs for a glass of wine. He said he would like that, so we sat and talked over some of the things that had taken place on the day of the funeral. Father Dave's personal attention allowed me to think others might continue filling my endless neediness with endless thoughtfulness.

Truly, I had no idea how grief works. I just knew it wasn't working the way it did in the black-and-white movies that constituted my early grief education. In the old movies I watched as a teen, grief went something like this: in receiving news that her fiancé has died in war, a leading lady orders her maid to draw the boudoir drapes and then dashes up a grand staircase to darkness and enclosure. From such movie scenes, I came to regard grief as either deadly or empowering. If it didn't wither a person into oblivion, it seemed to confer the authority to order people around.

But that was only Hollywood. In my estimation, I was interred with Mary ten miles to the west. "I died, too, but I have to go on living" are the words I used to describe my peculiar in-between position until, observing the alarm those words elicited, I stopped using them. In the post-funeral days, as it turned out, hardly anything was more real than the casseroles deposited on my front porch. I was still here on earth, there was no maid to pull my drapes, and daily life was going to have to go on pretty much as before.

On the Saturday after the funeral, Carol from All Saints Parish brought a chicken and broccoli casserole to which I ended up helping myself. After six days of eating next to nothing, I found the food delicious even if, by the third bite, it was tinged with guilt. How could I be enjoying anything on an afternoon with Mary so completely gone? But there it was: enjoyment. Thinking I had it in me to bake a chicken, I went to the grocery store on Monday morning. A friend who spotted me inspecting apples said, "I'm surprised to see you here."

"Well, Evelyn, it's one thing to grieve, but on an empty stomach? Never."

So I went home and baked a chicken that John and the kids ate. We chewed in silence, but the main thing was that we were together and wanted to be. Afterward we sat down, watched a television show, and laughed a little. It wasn't the show that gave relief; it was being in the room together. On that night and for many cold nights to come, I wanted one thing: to sit in a warm room with my family. When John and the kids were settled in plain view and looking more or less content, the fear inside me ebbed.

As I opened my eyes each morning, Mary catapulted into my mind and lodged there until day's end, causing me to perceive reality through her absence. Upon examining a cut-into coffee cake in the freezer, for example, I would think, "This looks like something Mary would have done. On the other side of this knife cut, she was alive." And I kept trying to buy groceries with her food preferences in mind, more than once removing her favorite yogurt from my shopping cart and putting it back on the shelf.

I noted the exact number of days that had passed without Mary and began telling myself things like, "One week ago, she was still alive. If I could turn the clock back ten days, everything would be different." Even at that, I wasn't feeling the full stab of her departure. "I really think I can get through this grief okay," I told one friend three days after the funeral, and "My mornings are eighty percent normal," I told someone else a week later.

A question arose with breakfast coffee: "What do I have to do to get through this day?" It was an estimate of the hurdles standing between me and nap time; and in this, my mother continued to give example. Downcast as she was, she was getting out of bed each day, pulling herself together, and going to her office-manager job as she had always done. If she could attempt a normal day at the age of seventy-five, what excuse did I have? Like her, I had to trust in the value of physically accomplishing things each day. As I came to see for myself, any movement toward routine, even the making of a peanut butter sandwich, was a movement away from despair.

Many days, John and I went to early Mass. For me, it wasn't so much to fulfill a Carmelite commitment as to fill a hole in life. It was not as though I could attend to the words of the homily; they quickly fell away. It wasn't that I could enter into the Mass thoughtfully; I was too distracted by thoughts of Mary. It was that, beyond all word and thought, I could still cup my hand and receive the Eucharist. I could open myself to an event that I knew to be restorative even though it felt ordinary. For a few minutes each day, I could hold John's hand and allow the people around me—the mothers with toddlers, the white-haired retirees, the businessmen and women, the students in green plaid uniforms—the whole diverse community, by virtue of its power and dignity, to carry me.

Some people went out of their way to talk with John and me on the sidewalk after Mass. One woman told us about the troubles she was having with her mentally disabled teenage daughter who was beginning to discover sex. Another person disclosed his struggle with major depression and suicidal thoughts, not so much for answers, I think, as for the acceptance he seemed to feel we could now offer.

Perhaps those sidewalk encounters were a gentle way for others to acknowledge our limitations by revealing theirs, but I perceived in them a connection I hadn't sensed before. Maybe a deep, invisible connection among parishioners had been in place all the decades of my life from the time of childhood, a communion of imperfect saints, and I just hadn't recognized it.

While praying the Liturgy of the Hours in the post-funeral days, I noticed psalms registering differently than before. The phrase from Psalm 146, "I will praise the Lord all my days, make music to my God while I live," which had once rolled pleasantly from my mouth now caught there. Make music to my God? I couldn't imagine what that might mean and had no interest in finding out. The proposal in Psalm 30 that God turns "mourning into dancing" likewise seemed dubious.

But I was coming to see that certain psalms, while shining a laser beam on suffering as they do, got under the grief like nothing else. At night prayer on Fridays, for example, I would pray from Psalm 88:

> I am reckoned as one in the tomb:
> I have reached the end of my strength,
> like one alone among the dead;
> like the slain lying in their graves;
> like those you remember no more. . . .

A few weeks before she died, Mary handed me a school paper to sign. "Mom," she said, "I am so alone."

"But you're not alone. You have us. You have your friends. You're never really alone. I mean, not really."

Saying nothing (who could fault her?), Mary took her signed paper and left. Only after she died did I recognize her terrible isolation in the phrases of Psalm 142:

> Look on my right and see:
> there is not one who takes my part.
> I have no means of escape,
> not one who cares for my soul.

Now, I shared Mary's isolation. I was akin to the Israelite exile of Psalm 137 who hung his harp in a poplar tree and sat down to weep by the rivers of Babylon: "O how could I sing the song of the Lord on alien soil?"[16] My careful life was alien to me, including my relationship with God, for whom I now maintained deference bordering on fear.

Five days after Mary's death, I tried to express in a journal entry the estrangement I was feeling: "A child, flesh of my flesh, has become part of the cool September earth. Dear God, how? I acknowledge your right to call her home as you wish. I acknowledge that she is best with you and at peace. What I want to know is, how am I supposed to live without her?"

But even if God hadn't wished to call her home, there existed a divine right to Mary's life that trumped my claim if, indeed, I ever had a claim. That much was clear to me. God was powerful and I, who could not save my daughter, was powerless. I was now expected to live with that reality, and it smoldered inside me. There was also the confounding reality of being married to a man with whom I passed along a susceptibility to mental illness. So, why *did* God bring John and me together in the first place? It was a question we asked aloud on one occasion and then brushed aside as unanswerable.

A few days after the funeral, I sat on a footstool in our dressing room and watched John loop the ends of his tie and tighten the knot as he had done for five thousand mornings. When the moment arrived for deciding upon shoes, though, he merely stared at the closet floor. At the wake, one of his colleagues had told me, "John should take a month off from his practice. He needs the time." He did need the time. But without partner or group, he could hardly afford to take a month off. Besides, he had a commitment to his patients, many of them elderly, who were already scheduled to see him. John also needed a schedule and the orderliness of a medical office. So I handed him the black loafers and pulled his gray jacket off the hanger. He looked polished and more or less ready.

"I hope things go well for you today," I said.

"Well, I need to get back to work. That's for sure." Maybe his patients and staff could draw him out and help him think about something other than losing Mary. Maybe that would prove impossible.

A little later that morning, Lauren got out of the car in the school parking lot and turned her head to smile at a classmate. I tried to believe she'd find a way to navigate the sixth grade without her big sister. When she came home from school in the afternoon, she told me she had waked that morning with immense sadness. That was all she would say about her first day back. As usual, she spread schoolbooks out on the floor and started her homework. After a few minutes, she sat down beside me on the couch and let me put my arm around her and touch her silky hair.

"I'm glad you can do your work," I said.

"Not doing it would just make things worse, Mom."

I began our favorite name game. "If Judy Garland married Howdy Doody, she'd be Judy Doody."

"No, if Geraldine Grogan married Hulk Hogan, she'd be Geraldine Grogan Hogan."

So it went until the cinder block sadness lifted and Lauren went out to bicycle with her friends Cindy and Beth. I could not comprehend her loss. Once when she was nine years old, she sneaked into Mary's room to put on makeup. I saw her leaving the room with lips and chin coated in maroon lipstick.

"Why did you do that?" I asked.

"Because I want to be like her." Embarrassed, she began to cry. She'd always admired her big sister but was now saying, "I don't want to be like Mary, ever." I understood that, but it troubled me. What emotional undercurrents was Lauren enduring and at what cost? I made a pediatric appointment for her. She was due for a physical but also needed the chance to talk privately with her doctor. Maybe he could then tell whether or not she was grieving normally for an eleven-year-old.

"She looks good, really growing fast now," Dr. Clark told me. Nearing her twelfth birthday, Lauren was looking more like a teen every day. "She's quiet, understandably, but everything checks out. Tell John if *he* ever wants to talk sometime, even gibberish, he should give me a call. I do gibberish."

After that exchange, I continued to feel anxious about Lauren because I had no idea what might be going on inside her. Even when we sat at Kline's Drive-In eating ice cream dip-tops after school, to my mind a perfect place for calling a spade a spade, Lauren would say little about what she'd gone through that day. John and I began to think she needed professional help in finding her voice.

When I asked Dr. Matthews what course she thought we should take with Lauren, she said, "With your family history, I'd advise a child psychiatrist. I know a good one."

A day later, I took her advice and called Dr. Sims. "I don't want Lauren to have to be the strong one. Her father and I want her to be able to say . . . whatever. She's going to school every day and doing her work. She has plenty of friends, and she's always on the phone. But she's not able to say too much about what's going on inside."

"First of all, please know how sorry I am about your daughter's death. There's no worse trauma for a family than what you're experiencing. And you're right about Lauren. It's not that denial is a bad thing. It's just that, as time goes on, it takes more and more energy to maintain. Then it becomes a real problem."

Lauren began meeting with Dr. Sims each week for an hour after school. From the start, she hated it. Dr. Sims tried to get her to draw a picture of Mary and describe what she'd been like. He tried to get her to talk about her friends, her schoolwork, John Paul, her parents, vacations, our cat, Mama—anything at all—but Lauren resisted. Even though we explained there was nothing wrong with her and that she only needed to talk to Dr. Sims, she said little and resented much.

Just the same, John and I didn't want to repeat the mistake we'd made with Mary by assuming that Lauren's private thoughts, no matter what, would eventually prove benign. I prayed for wisdom and urged Lauren to give Dr. Sims a chance. Obedient as always, she did try. She met with him every week for six months, and though she never said the therapy was helpful, we hoped someday she might see it as helpful. That she was crushed beyond words was more than any of us, including Dr. Sims, could grasp.

MARY, LAUREN, AND JOHN PAUL, 1988

John Paul was having only a slightly better time with Dr. Matthews whom he began seeing twice a week. To reduce stress, he withdrew from classes at George Mason University for the fall semester. Even on a higher dose of tranquillizing medication, however, he remained agitated. He told us he couldn't sleep in the house. He said he'd rather sleep in the garage in his Toyota; that we bothered him. The only solution John and I could come up with was having him stay in my parents' spare bedroom for a few nights. "Of course," my mother said when I asked her.

That arrangement worked for a while, but John Paul was home most of the time anyway, just walking the house in grief. He said that moving through the living room and dining room, into the kitchen, down the hall, and back again, over and over, was calming. Maybe it was calming to him, but it was disturbing to me who could hear his pounding footsteps no matter where I was in the house.

He came by my bedroom one afternoon and leaned against the door frame with his hands in his jean pockets, looking more relaxed than usual. "I've been thinking about Mary. She didn't know how to protect herself, Mom. When I was in Miami, I learned how to protect myself. But Mary didn't know how."

"What do you mean?"

"Well, people can be hard. You have to be able to protect yourself, and Mary didn't know how."

"No, she didn't. But all she had to do was say three words—just three words—and *we* would've protected her. If she'd just said, 'I need help,' we'd have had her in the hospital within an hour. She did *not* have to do what she did."

"Of course not."

"You wouldn't do what Mary did, would you?"

"No! I would never do that."

I believed him; John Paul had always been emotionally honest with me in a way Mary had not. Besides, I had to believe him. I couldn't lie awake at night waiting for an ominous sound, and I couldn't go into a sustained cringe every time he left the house. What I could do was call upon God for John Paul's safety. I could couple the advice of my mother to that of my husband. "Try to live as normally as you can," my mother said.

"You should continue with school," John said. "It makes no sense for you to quit."

Despite my reluctance to leave John Paul alone for hours at a time, I agreed with John. I did need to keep going to school. It was one of the good things in my life. It was where I could look for answers about Mary.

Endnotes

12 Andre Dubus, *Meditations from a Movable Chair* (New York: Vintage Books, 1998), 85.

13 Emily Dickinson, *The Complete Poems of Emily Dickinson*, ed. Thomas H. Johnson (Boston: Little, Brown and Company, 1961), 162.

14 W. H. Auden, "Funeral Blues," *Poems* (New York: Alfred A. Knopf, 1995), 50.

15 "Order for the Blessing of a Family," *Book of Blessings* (Collegeville, MN: The Liturgical Press, 1989), 8, 9.

16 Psalms 146, 30, 88, 142, 137, *Christian Prayer: The Liturgy of the Hours* (New York: Catholic Book Publishing Co., 1976), 961, 755, 1052-3, 703, 954.

5

BEING SCHOOLED

Although sometimes it seems life would be much easier and much less painful
if all humans were born totally awake, they are not.
CLARISSA PINKOLA ESTÉS[17]

So from slumber, we awake to attend.
BERNARD LONERGAN[18]

AT TEN O'CLOCK ON SUNDAY night after the funeral, I began putting my notes in order for Monday morning Christology class. Shuffling papers for several minutes was getting me nowhere; but I felt if I just showed up for class, everything would work out. I was confident in the willingness of other people to help me through the rough spots as they had been doing for days. It was a new way of relating. On the day before Mary died, for instance, when I told my mother I had fallen in the street while jogging that morning, she asked who'd picked me up. "Are you kidding? I picked myself up. If I had to wait for someone to pick me up, I'd be waiting a long time."

Now here I was a week later with a sheaf of unread assignments in my lap. I had fallen behind in a fast-moving course, and though self-reliance had been drummed into me from childhood, it wasn't going to get me through the next morning. Others would have to pick me up; and I believed they would do so rather quickly.

Our classroom was a no-frills arrangement of thirty desks, two blackboards, and a crucifix. It was taught by a red-headed priest whose heels clacked on the wooden teaching platform as he paced back and forth while lecturing. Father Bowen used humor, sometimes sarcasm, to lower the tension of delivering precise, orthodox ideas about Jesus Christ in such a way that they could be exactly understood. On the first day of class in August he had said, "If any of you think we're going to sit in a circle, hold hands, and talk about what Jesus means to us, you should leave right now." No one left.

"What we're going to do," he said, "is to address Christ's own question, 'Who do people say that I am?' How did the followers of the *man* Jesus come to claim his universal significance? And how do we go about making that claim? 'Who do you say that I am?' is more than an academic question; it's a journey of faith. And we're probably going to have to deconstruct some of your ideas about Jesus along the way."

There was nothing comfortable about the class—quite the opposite. It was intimidating. We had hundreds of pages of readings to deal with for the midterm examination in October that consisted in a thirty-minute conversation with Father Bowen from which there was no escape. Judging by the earnestness of their questions, the Franciscan, Augustinian, and Carmelite seminarians were at home in the subject matter. Religious sisters, with silver hair and youthful faces, who were on sabbatical, seemed delighted to be in the class. Then there were people like me who felt called to attempt a master's degree in theology without being able to say why.

But I could say this: on a January evening eight months earlier when I'd merged into a ribbon of interstate taillights and headed to my very first foundational theology class, I wasn't trying to prove anything. I did wonder why I was leaving a husband and three children at home, driving forty miles to Takoma Park, Maryland, and spending $1,200 on a class. But the gamble seemed worth taking.

The first thing Professor Manning did that January night was hand out pounds of required readings she'd copied, collated, and stapled. Students whistled and whispered as papers rose inches high on their desks. I was caught between fear at the prospect of being in over my head and delight at being taken seriously by a professor who would not be watering down the material for the lay students.

That first class focused on human transcendence, the intuition shared by all of us regarding the "more" in human existence, the "something more" that we can never entirely grasp. The idea wasn't foreign. Twenty years before when John Paul was a baby, I was feeding him breakfast one morning when a single thought wafted in: *There must be more to life than this.*

My "this" happened to be pretty good. I had a new marriage, a beautiful son, a nice home. While not in the least unhappy—in fact, happier than ever—I sensed a reality underneath the reality I was living each day. Spooning cereal into John Paul that morning, I perceived something fine and uplifting that I could not take hold of, something just below the surface of dailiness, something that endowed every midnight feeding and baked dinner potato with meaning. It was that very "something," I believed, that had led me to Professor Martha Manning's class.

She said we'd be dealing with modern atheism and the problem of evil and human freedom. We would discuss whether or not God makes contact with humans through revelation. "You can't see this now," she said, "but the syllabus has logic to it, and it'll come together for you."

I believed in that possibility; I just wasn't sure I could manage the complicated work. She referred to one of the readings and noted: "The phrase 'spirit in the world' is the key to understanding that whole piece, so remember that as you're reading."

Dazzled, I turned to the Irish Christian Brother seated behind me and said, "She's really a teacher's teacher, isn't she?"

Leading us into the strange new world of theology while taking time to highlight a tiny phrase for our benefit—well, I'd never seen another teacher so adept at shoring up grand ideas with little gestures of concern for her students. Getting in the car after class, I made up my mind to give the course everything I could give it. Then I dialed up a 1960s rock and roll station and sang most of the way back to Manassas.

Throughout the winter of 1995, foundational theology was an exhilaration that called forth effort of a kind I was unused to making. "I have to study an hour or two *every day* just to stay afloat," I would tell people. "If I don't, I will *sink*." The class required reflection and discourse about the ways God relates to our individual days on earth and was, in that way, preparing me for the suicide and God questions lying just ahead.

On April 19, 1995, as Professor Manning was constructing our exam, Timothy McVeigh and Terry Nichols blew up the Alfred P. Murrah Federal Building in Oklahoma City, killing 168 people and injuring 800. That act of terror became part of our exam. "In a parish address for adults, what would you say about the senseless suffering in Oklahoma City?"

With only a few days to answer, I became my father. He would stomp around the house each April 14, gathering information for income taxes, and we kids knew better than to bother him. But my daughter Mary wasn't put off by the agitation. She seemed intrigued. As I was sitting at the word processor one night, she came up behind me and touched the top of my head. "How's it going, Mom?"

"Okay. I've finally got some of the questions figured out. Things like, 'What kind of person could bomb children?' And, 'Where is God?'" Once I figure out the answers, I'll be all done. Yeah, right."

"Well, good luck with that," she said with a smile. "I want to read it when you're finished." Maybe she was just trying to be supportive; and maybe she was looking for clarity about God and death even then, five months before she died.

In a way, I hope she wasn't looking to me for theological clarity. My exam essays were rudimentary, accurate to an extent but mainly superficial. "God is here to console and help when bombs destroy the innocent," I wrote. "God does enter into the mess we humans make." It didn't occur to me to ask why the innocent have to suffer bombs in the first place. Instead, I ended up pointing to the symbol of the cross that "seems to show God saying, 'This is absolute evil which cannot be denied. But out of great love, I have made it good.'"

It was a tidy answer that worked on an exam but failed in life. It took only a couple of weeks from the time of Mary's death to know the deficiency of that answer. By then, all I could do was stand in my bedroom shouting to both God and Mary, "I *hate* it that you're gone!"

As to the kind of person who could bomb children, my answer fell even shorter. Writing mostly about the human freedom to choose who we shall be before God, I trotted out theological theories of behavior to get light on McVeigh's and Nichols's horrible decision. Evil behavior was, in my telling, mostly about theories and decisions.

Professor Manning did not let those inadequacies go unremarked. In the margins of my exam paper she wrote, "Some acknowledgment should be given to the issue of whether or not certain people are so distorted (blinded) by their environment or experiences that their freedom is diminished radically—almost eradicated. It is a question with which we must deal."

It was a question with which I would soon be dealing night and day, weighing my daughter's horrible decision to end her life over against the obvious diminishment of her freedom. But as the semester came to an end in April 1995, all I could think about was my attraction to theology and whether I should continue studying it.

In August my family decided to escape brick-oven heat by heading to Lake Placid in the Adirondacks. We knew we needed fun. In addition to the college visits Mary and I were making, she had worked most summer nights as hostess at the North China Inn near home. For his part, John was putting in eighty-hour weeks with his patients. That was nothing new. What was new, with the advent of managed care, were the boxes of paperwork he brought home on the weekends, the hiring of additional secretaries to file insurance claims, and the creeping uncertainty about the survival of his twenty-year medical practice. The adjustments he was forced to make set an anxious tone around the house.

"But," he said as we packed the car to leave, "this is probably our last family vacation, so we should enjoy it." He was only talking about Mary leaving for college the following year, but the remark made me sad.

Standing at the kitchen sink on the morning of our vacation departure, I worried out loud about John Paul and Mary. Their young lives should have been moving forward but seemed to be stalling. John Paul had begun pacing throughout the house that summer because he didn't know what else to do. For him and for me, it was unnerving to the point of tears; and aside from an extra pill here and there, Dr. Matthews had nothing to offer.

Mary liked her restaurant hostess job and came home animated with stories every night, but her sleep pattern was unraveling. I was afraid she'd have to go back on the antidepressant Prozac she'd been taken off when school ended two months earlier. The delicacy of her mental wiring was becoming more noticeable, and it troubled me.

Still, I buried those anxieties as we piled into the Custom Cruiser station wagon and headed to New York State. When we arrived at the High Peaks Wilderness Area near Lake Placid the following day, we began winding up Cascade Mountain into sunlight filtering through oaks. Along the roadside, leaves glowed in the slanting light, which held all the faith, hope, and love I needed. John Paul was in front with me; and John, Mary, and Lauren were in back, quiet and captivated. We were all together and going someplace magical.

Part of our time together at Lake Placid did turn out to be placid. The kids stood in man-made snow on an August evening and then ice skated near the rink on which the miracle on ice took place at the 1980 Olympics. A couple of days later, on the Feast of the Assumption, we all walked to Mass at St. Agnes Church and then to dinner in Lake Placid Village. That was the best, an evening I would choose a hundred times out of a hundred.

But there was also the day Mary became furious with me for taking a picture of her sitting in a paddleboat on Mirror Lake. She thought I was making fun of her, and her misperception both puzzled and hurt me. There was also the moment I saw her lying on the bed reading *Ivanhoe,* assigned summer reading for which she was going to be tested. Glaring at the page, she seemed completely unfocused, even absent. It was the same distracted look I'd seen on John Paul's face when he'd struggled with his studies, and it set off a depth charge in me. *She's never going to be able to finish that book. She's gone someplace in her mind that I can't reach, and I can hardly breathe.*

A morning or two later, John and I were sitting underneath a mounted moose head in a hunter's restaurant, eating pancakes. "This makes no sense," I said, "but I want to take another theology class this fall—Christology." John lifted his coffee mug. "I should probably just get a job to help with Mary's college expenses. But I really want to study theology, maybe even try for a master's degree." Then, to my surprise, I began to cry.

John looked directly at me, his eyes soft. "Well, why not? It must mean a lot to you. Why don't you just go ahead and take Christology?"

He didn't ask what I intended to do with a master's degree or where the money would come from. He didn't ask how I would make time to study. Of the tears, he made no mention. I couldn't have explained them anyway. Only years later did I see them as a signal of profound distress for John Paul and Mary who were ill and fading just as I was reaching for new life. But I won't deny the frustration in my tears that morning.

MARJ AND JOHN ON THEIR TWENTY-THIRD WEDDING ANNIVERSARY, 1995.

So there I was in Christology class six Monday mornings later, resuming my new life. While I was setting up my tape recorder on the desk, a couple of religious sisters came over and hugged me. Still proud of my daughter, I pulled out a photograph of her wearing her black prom dress against a backdrop of April forsythia.

"What a beautiful girl . . . ," said one older sister, pressing her eyes closed.

"I've been praying—we've all been praying—for your family," another said. "And don't worry about the handouts you missed. I got copies for you."

Having heard the news, young seminarians in jeans began crowding around to see the photograph. Maybe they wanted to look at the face of someone who had actually done the unthinkable. Because their interest seemed to keep Mary alive for a few seconds, I didn't pull the photo back. *She looks normal, don't you think? Would it be okay with you if I curled up on the floor in a fetal position?*

"I know how you feel," one sister said. "I spent six months taking care of my father who was 85. He just passed away. So, yes, I know what it's like."

I wanted to tell her she did *not* know what it was like, but Father Bowen walked in at that moment. He glanced my way for an instant without saying anything. For that I was thankful. He may not even have known who I was, but I didn't care. If he had said anything to me, I would have wept and run out of the room and missed the class. I considered his silence a grant of privacy. It provided an outpost from which I could begin to reclaim my shaky student self.

After printing "Kingdom of God" on the board, he said, "The kingdom of God, or reign of God, is the center of Jesus' teaching. He didn't go around proclaiming himself. He proclaimed that the reign of God was beginning to take place through him."

The idea was not unfamiliar; I'd heard it declared for years. Until that morning, however, I had not known myself to be in such need of God's reign. Bowen was telling me that Jesus' forgiveness and compassion invited all people, *especially* the marginalized and outcast, into God's kingdom. Without using my daughter's name, he seemed to be speaking directly about her.

"Jesus proclaimed the reign of God mostly through parables," Bowen said. Writing "shock," "seduce," and "challenge" on the board, he said, "At the heart of each parable is a metaphor. Metaphors bring together two realities that don't belong together, so they scandalize us. They shock our imagination. They upend our world. They seduce us into new insight. Metaphors challenge us to make a new decision about how we're going to live according to the reign of God."

Then he made a remark I never suspected could be true: "If someone is open to the jolt that a parable delivers, the reign of God can be made present to that person." Just days before, I had been jolted. My world had been upended by two realities that, pushed together, had shocked and continued to shock me: Mary and suicide. Might that clash hold forth the hope of God breaking into my life?

No answer came to me during that Monday morning class, but I figured this much: Bowen hadn't spoken about the reign of God just to make me feel better my first day back—hardly. He spoke about the possibility of God's reign in our lives because, after decades of theological scholarship, he found it credible. That was what, in the end, made me feel better.

After class, I went into the Union's darkened chapel where a Mass in memory of my daughter was about to begin. A dozen or so students and faculty were filling in, among them Professor Manning who took my hand, told me how sorry she was, and sat down beside me. There was no use trying to hide my tears any longer, so I put my head down and cried. As self-conscious as an adolescent, I wanted to slink away. But slinking was impossible in such an intimate setting, and I knew it was impossible when a woman behind me touched my shoulder lightly to comfort me.

It was October 2, the feast day of the Guardian Angels, those messengers sent "to light and guard, rule and guide" each human being along the way of life. Just as the celebrant reminded us that guardian angels are manifestations of God's love, I sensed my daughter's gentle presence right beside me on the bench, not as an angel but as herself. Looking up to the highest peak of the chapel ceiling, I breathed her in and believed, not for the first time that she was all right with God and God was all right with her.

I wanted to get home to see that everyone else in the family was all right. The last time I'd come in from the District of Columbia was eight days prior when John and I had found Mary on her bed. The thought of walking back into the house after a trip to the District made my hands clammy. But as soon as I came through the door, John Paul greeted me with a smile. He'd been at All Saints that morning helping one of the secretaries. While not exactly energetic, he seemed stable enough. *Not bad. John Paul seems okay; there are no messages from John or Lauren. It looks as though we might make it.*

Having taken time out of their workday, my mother and sister stepped in through the backdoor and, trying to look cheerful, sat down with me. Both wore dark skirts and shoes, their hair styled, their faces made up. They seemed composed to meet the day's obligations.

"How was school today?" Joy asked.

I said it had gone well. Evidently, that was what they'd come over to hear because after that, they fell quiet. Neither spoke of her private pain, but their eyes glistened with tears. Differences of opinion that had once tugged at us faded to unimportance in that moment.

Normally, my mother would have asked, "Where's Mary?" It was the question she always asked. Then I would have gone to the bottom of the stairs and called for Mary to come down and be with us, and joining us, she would have made us all happier. But deprivation drifted in the air like incense. We ended up talking about our day's comings and goings throughout which I saw my mother and sister as cheerleaders, albeit somber ones, who had been rooting for me. While I had my eyes on John Paul and Lauren, my mother and sister had their eyes on me. They were letting me know it was all right to go on with life, a powerful endorsement from two women whose judgment I valued.

Picking up a handful of unopened mail, I said, "Look at all these cards. It's been this way since last week; something like twenty-five cards a day."

"Well, I tell you," my mother said, "I could hardly get out of church yesterday for all the people coming up to me. Dr. Anderson mentioned Mary in his sermon. He talked about all of us and the hurt he'd seen in our eyes."

Eighty years before, when my mother's grandfather James fatally shot himself in rural Georgia, he was not mentioned in any sermon. The cause of his death was never spoken. Though the townspeople of Rockville probably figured out what had happened, no one approached family members after church with condolence. But now, views about suicide had changed enough that my mother could get support denied *her* mother, Sarah, James's daughter—my grandmother—who it seemed to me carried unspent grief to the end of her days.

After my mother and sister left, I started opening the big envelopes piled on the coffee table. They contained hardback cards, announcing that Mary had been enrolled in one or another spiritual society of the Roman Catholic Church in order to share in its Masses, prayers, and good works, sometimes perpetually. There was the Union of Prayer of the Discalced Carmelite Friars as well as the Marian Spiritual Alliance. There was the St. Patrick's Missionary Circle along with the De Sales Seminary Associates and the Sacred Heart Spiritual Society. People all over the world were praying for my daughter out of their goodness, I believed, but also out of the moral seriousness with which they regarded her suicide.

Several Mass cards spoke for "repose of the soul" of Mary Antus. At a particular parish on a specific date, a priest would be saying, "This Mass is being offered in memory of Mary Antus." Most of the Mass cards came from parishioners, but John's Protestant patients sent them, too, along with Mary's high school friends. Fifty such Masses would eventually be offered all over the Arlington Diocese for the repose of her soul, an upwelling of highest prayer, the sacrifice of the Mass.

I had grown up as a Methodist and believed that the newly deceased go straight to heaven, but joining the Catholic Church required me to rethink that belief. While studying the topic of "purgation" for my parish inquiry class eighteen years earlier, I had underlined two thoughts: purgatory is an encounter with God after death in which we see God as God really is and ourselves as we really are, both sinful and graced. Second, purgatory is a passage through the purifying fire of God's love.

With its emphasis not only on God's saving love but also human love reaching past death, the Catholic Church's teaching about purgatory made sense to me. My love for Mary had been expressed before in concrete ways, such as buying her new shoes when she'd outgrown the old. Now that I had no place to put that love, I could nevertheless kneel at Mass, pray for her, and trust that she was benefiting. That was what I could do.

In card after pastel card, people said they were praying for Mary and our family. They usually began with an admission of helplessness which, condensed, could have read: "Experience has taught me there is little anyone can do or say to ease the pain . . . words are totally inadequate . . . they can't express how we ache for you . . . we wish we could be there in person to comfort you . . . Roger cries." Inside my protective numbness, I couldn't feel their sorrow; it flowed away from me. But I recognized the lament in their words and their effort not to be glib. Even the aunt who reminded me that no one is promised a long, happy life began by saying she loved us and hurt for us.

"You're in my thoughts and prayers" was the reassurance nearly everyone offered. One person wrote, "Our hearts go out to you," and another, "We stand with you in your sorrow." Neighbors, friends, cousins, and even John's patients responded bodily to Mary's death by allowing our pain into their beings and sending their hearts into us. The graciousness of that exchange made me shake my head in wonder.

A note from the principal of Mary's high school quoted St. Francis de Sales on the subject of death and God's providence:

> Let us walk with great confidence under the standard of God's providence without yielding to fears that might trouble us. If we think of death with uneasiness, the thought will be more injurious than advantageous to us. Let us think on it with peace and tranquility of mind, reposing in the bosom of Providence. . . . Provided I accomplish His Most Holy Will, what else have I to do but abandon myself to His Providence . . . [19]

97

But I was incapable of walking with great confidence that day. I *was* yielding to fears and thinking of Mary's death with uneasiness. After the Christology lecture about God's reign breaking in on human shocks and jolts, how was I supposed to think of Mary's death with peace and tranquility? I'd felt my daughter's presence at Mass a couple of hours before, but I knew her suicide had not accomplished his most holy will and that coming to peace about it was not going to be easy.

Father Kieran from the Carmelite monastery offered pastoral guidance: "There are many things that happen in God's providence that we cannot understand, but we can always trust in Him and know that in His wisdom, He knows how to bring good out of everything. This we will see only in glory."

It was comforting in its way, the idea that God is in charge and will ultimately make the bewildering realities of life come clear. But, again, how was I to think of suicide as part of God's providence? Had Mary been destined for a miserable life from which God decided to swoop in and save her? I couldn't see what possible good could ever be better than having her here with us. Those uncertainties wore away at me even as I told myself, "God knows best," and tried to believe it. Even so, I was coming to prefer the uncertainties to what were, in my estimation, nice platitudes.

Three sympathy cards on the coffee table provided what amounted to character sightings of Mary that otherwise would have been lost to me. "I had the pleasure of teaching Mary for two years," her French teacher wrote. "In her quiet way she brought much to the classroom—she liked French, applied herself, and was always positive and helpful to others. She had so much to offer so many . . ."

A mother of one of Mary's high school friends wrote, "Our family had the pleasure of meeting Mary last year. I remember so clearly the night she came to our house. She stood and talked with me in the kitchen, and out of all the kids, I remember her. When my daughter transferred into the high school midyear, Mary ate lunch with her and made her feel welcome."

I could see Mary making polite talk with that mother while her friends partied in the basement. I could imagine her getting up from her cafeteria table and sitting down with a new student. Since childhood, it seemed, she had tried to be kind to those she thought needed it most.

"Whenever we were together in a family setting," my brother, George, wrote, "Mary and I would find a quiet moment and share something funny—a joke or comment on the unfolding scene. We would be the only ones who knew, and afterward we would just have to look at each other to reignite the mirth." Though it was hard to recall Mary's laughter as ever having been "inviting, warm, rich, and spontaneous," that is how George described it.

Before I could finish opening all the cards, a neighbor I hardly knew arrived with a warm banana-nut loaf. We sat on the sofa and had a piece. Maybe it was the friendliness of sitting on the sofa beside Barbara, enjoying a piece of the bread, or maybe it was my need to look dutiful, but I began telling her about our plans for family grief counseling. When she smiled, I lowered my fork, looked into her eyes, and said, "What would it be like to decide to die? I mean, can you imagine? What must it be like at the moment you cross that line and decide you're really going to do it? One moment, maybe you will and maybe you won't; and the next moment, you're going to do it. What on earth must that be like? I can't imagine."

Barbara looked at the floor for an instant and then back at me, as she said, "Marj, I think it would be a good idea if you went ahead with the counseling you mentioned."

Her words wilted me. If nice Barbara could put a stop to my musings, the grief rules had changed without my knowing it. During the week of the funeral, people had deferred to my every utterance. They had allowed me to talk and talk, and all that talking had helped me sort out my thoughts and connect with those people at a deeper level, or so I felt. Now Barbara seemed to be saying I was in a place unlike her place and that while I needed someone to talk to, it wasn't going to be her.

When I spoke about the thank-you notes I had yet to write, she said, "Please don't send me a thank-you note for this banana-nut bread."

I said I wouldn't, but I should have been thanking her for waking me up. I was inside a labyrinth of grief from which no amount of neighbor talk could rescue me. Yes, I needed grief counseling, but what I needed even more was my daughter. I couldn't stop thinking about her, and I was desperate to find her again.

Endnotes

17 Clarissa Pinkola Estés, *Women Who Run with the Wolves* (New York: Ballantine Books, 1995), 43.

18 Bernard Lonergan, *Method in Theology* (Toronto: University of Toronto Press, 1971), 13.

19 St. Francis de Sales, *Consoling Thoughts of St. Francis de Sales: On Sickness and Death* (New York: TAN Books, 2013), 64.

6

UNTANGLING

All of us are mysteries to ourselves, our most familiar mystery.
The question that each of us asks, the question that each of us is,
endures. . . .
ANNE E. CARR[20]

I STARTED LOOKING FOR MARY in her journals. She left nine
of them stacked in her closet and one on her desk, many of
them spiral-bound with loose paper shreds, their covers full of
scribbled phone numbers and lipstick brand names. Mary received her first journal as a Christmas present in 1985 when she
was eight years old. Inside the front cover I wrote, "Dear Mary,
please fill this little book with your good thoughts. Love, Mom."

Underneath my inscription she added, "The adventures of
Mary Kathryn Antus—Ha Ha, very funny." A few months later,
she had started filling the book with neat, third-grade block
print. When she needed a word she didn't know how to spell,
she spelled it phonetically and kept writing. For almost ten
years, she wrote her account of daily life. Though she might
sit with John and me in the evening and watch a movie, she often brought along a notebook. Anyone who spent time with her

came to see the concentration she poured onto paper. As I was later to learn from her suicide note, she wrote right to the end of her life. It was her last act.

However ragtag Mary's notebooks had grown over the years, however fragmentary they might prove to be, they were now gold. I picked up the bulky journal lying on her desk. *Mary was a smart girl. If she hadn't wanted me to read this, she would've pitched it into a dumpster.* That was my rationale for reading private thoughts that, out of respect, I had never read. But Mary was in the notebook, and I wanted to have her words run through my head once again so I could make believe she was still with me. And after getting her back with me, I wanted to find out what was going through her mind at the very end.

Starting with the last entry on Thursday, September 21, I searched for clues. Three days before her death she wrote: "I'm so sick and frustrated of life in general. I'm never smart enough. I'm never funny enough. My clothes aren't right. I can't drive well. My handwriting is messy. I don't have a boy-friend. . . . At school I feel so alone. Every day, I'm truly on my own. I know plenty of nice people to say 'hello' to in the halls, but that's about where it ends. I have no plans. I want to die. Soon." In the next paragraph she wrote: "Somehow, I'll just have to survive this. It's not too late to have a happy childhood, is it? (Yeah.)"

Something inside me turned over. I headed for my bed-room rocking chair where I sat down and shut my eyes against the evidence I had encountered. In five words—"I want to die. Soon."—she had marked the precise wrap-up of her life.

Still, that fatal mood was not the one I witnessed on the day Mary actually wrote those words. As I recalled, Lauren had come into my bedroom on the evening of September 21 complaining about a math problem that, after attempting to help her with, I realized was beyond my ability. "Go get Mary," I said, so Lauren called to Mary to come join us. She came promptly, sat down on the floor with Lauren, and got her to settle down and focus on the problem. Together they found a solution. To my eyes that night, Mary was a devoted sister who, in showing the patience of a kindergarten teacher, did something admirable. How could she have written that she wanted to die on the very day she showed such know-how and affection?

When Mary came home the next day from what would be her last day of school, a Friday, she slipped into my bedroom and lay down on the bed beside me as I read the newspaper. Because her senior class picture had been scheduled for that day, she was not wearing her khaki school uniform but, instead, a simple black dress with gold earrings, her dark hair glossy and sleek. She didn't smile much that afternoon, but she did look pulled together, stylish and lovely. Those were the qualities that drew me. When she turned on her side facing me and propped her head in her hand, I looked into her deep brown eyes. "Thanks for helping Lauren last night. You'd be a good teacher someday. Ever thought about it?"

Gazing right through me, she didn't acknowledge the compliment or answer the question. She seemed weary, not impolite, and I let the subject drop. I really didn't have the heart for it anyway. She'd been taking a new dose of antidepressant Prozac and Nortriptyline for only a couple of weeks and, as I understood it, probably needed a couple more weeks to begin feeling better. *Go easy, keep it light, don't overwhelm her.* So she and I talked randomly for an hour about haircuts, rainy weather, and the approach of my sister's birthday. When I showed her some makeup brushes I'd gotten that morning, she showed me how they were to be used. She was altogether agreeable, and nothing in her demeanor suggested the darkness of her thoughts.

I could see that enthusiasm had dropped out of Mary's personality, yes, but I did not grasp the significance of what I was seeing. I sensed her frailty, but sensing it made me jittery, not protective, and the most I was capable of offering that afternoon was chitchat. I thought pleasant conversation would make a difference. I really thought that, in time, medication would bring Mary back around; and I really thought we had the time. I didn't suspect that the daughter lying two feet away from me was hounded from within and sick unto death and in urgent need of a hospital.

She followed me into the kitchen as I started dinner, and while waiting for the pasta water to boil, I sat down with her. With sunlight fading on a tranquil Friday evening, Mary asked the question of her life: "Mom, what's a GED?"

"I think it means General Educational Development. It's a program for people who haven't finished high school. But Mary, surely you're not . . . surely you want to graduate with your class. I mean, GED isn't the way to go. You know?"

Part of me was getting it, but part of me, the danger-response part, was not functioning. I understood the question to be about her; I did not comprehend its seriousness. Or maybe I sensed its seriousness and then shied away like a pony. Maybe I was too scared to conceive of my daughter as sick. She looked too good, for one thing, and she still showed common sense and savvy.

Not only that, she had come through for me over the past three years as the mature "oldest" child in the wake of John Paul's illness, and I was invested in seeing her as healthy. Having two children with mental illness didn't fit my worldview. My world barely had room for one sick child, not two, and especially not two at the same time. Having accepted the commonplace that God does not lay upon us burdens too heavy to carry, I told myself Mary couldn't be grievously ill, certainly not like John Paul, because such an illness would be unbearable and, circularly speaking, God does not ask the unbearable.

I was confused. In mid-September when I had asked Mary if she wanted to get a haircut before sitting for her senior portraits, she replied vaguely, "No, I don't want to get my hair cut anymore." The comment puzzled me, but I shrugged it off. After all, she'd been making her way well enough through the first three weeks of school. She left on time each morning, brought a backpack full of books home each afternoon, and even consulted with me a couple of times about assignments. On her own initiative, she signed up for the College Board exams slated for October.

But on that Friday evening in the kitchen when Mary had asked about the GED, Lauren observed something she told me about years later. She said that Mary bit her lip when I remarked that the GED was not a good option. I didn't see her bite her lip, and even if I had, I wouldn't have thought anything of it.

In truth, to break through to me that evening, Mary would have had to grab me by the shoulders, look me in the eyes, and say in plain language that she couldn't take another day of school and wasn't going back on Monday. That would have gotten my attention. That would have gotten me to ask, really ask, what was going on in her life. It would've gotten John and me talking to each other and to her. It would have prompted a phone call to Dr. Matthews, and more than likely, it would have saved Mary's life.

But Mary was never one to show her feelings; she was never one to argue or slam doors or burst into tears. She walked out of the kitchen without saying anything more. I think that was the moment she gave up on me as someone who could help her. As for me, I went on to boil linguine in the comforting illusion that, despite my uneasiness, I had related well to my daughter that afternoon.

MARY, UNCLE GEORGE, AND GRANDMOTHER JOYCE AFTER MARY'S PERFORMANCE IN *KISS ME, KATE* WITH THE MIDDLEBURG PLAYERS, 1988.

Flipping back in Mary's journal six months to April 1, 1995, I did see some optimism: "Well, here we are. I've made it to yet another spring. It's getting warmer; everything is beginning to bloom. My depression that has plagued me all year seems to have lifted, and I may even be able to buckle down and salvage what's left of this year. Senior year looms on the horizon, and colleges are trying to 'woo' me, as my mother would say. I actually feel motivated in that regard, and I'm liking French more and more."

In the next paragraph, however, she wrote that her social life turned upside down after breaking up with her boyfriend, Tim, three weeks earlier. Leafing through the journal from beginning to end, I saw his name in most entries, and along with his name I saw phrases such as "hurt me," "angered me," "ignored me," and "persecuted me." The truth is, it was Mary who had broken up with Tim, not the other way around. Looking somewhat proud of herself, she told me she'd done the right thing. From what I knew of Tim, she *had* done the right thing. But now it wrenched her, and her journal was filled with pining for someone who no longer wanted any part of her. "I feel like if I jumped off a cliff," she wrote five days before her death, "no one would miss me. Tim is . . . perfectly happy without me."

I did a reality check: Wasn't what Mary had gone through with this boy something we all go through as teenagers? Who hasn't endured the agony of a breakup? What if everybody who'd loved and lost decided to die? We'd all be dead, that's what.

Closing the notebook, I placed it at the back of my closet in a cardboard box with Mary's other notebooks. Then I went into the garage and started the lawn mower, appreciative of its roar. I rode up and down the lawn, shearing autumn grass. Looking over my shoulder at the path I'd cut, I believed for a moment that my life made some kind of sense, that it was solid and real, and that not everything about it was disturbing.

Still, the journals lured me. Every day for weeks, I picked one out of the box and read for a few moments. People warned me not to. Mary's friend Kelli told me that, as a journal writer herself, she had scribbled a lot of nonsense over the years and that I shouldn't take every little thing Mary wrote as absolute truth. I understood her point, but it didn't dissuade me. Some people hinted I'd be better off just putting all the notebooks away, maybe even burning them, and moving on with my life, as though that were possible. I ignored those suggestions. What Mary had written I simply had to read.

I went back to that last journal, two qualities of which touched me especially. The first was Mary's effort to grow. On July 5, she titled one page "Aspirations for Summer of '95" and listed the following: "Work at North China Inn, lose weight (3 lbs. a month), learn how to type, keep up the French, keep up math, visit colleges (decide where to apply), work on college applications (essays, etc.), preregister for SAT I and SAT II, clean out closets, throw away things, give extra clothes to Salvation Army, take self-defense class, touch up the paint in my room, wax floor, turn mattress, READ A LOT, save money." If her check marks meant anything, she met quite a few of those summer aspirations.

On the facing page, she laid out a daily plan: "Exercise, pray, read and write, do chores, do job, practice typing, work on college applications, study French." In her quiet way as far as I could tell, she followed her plan. Her lists showed how much she cared about her life and how, working against frustration and internal strain, she tried to make it whole. Anyone reading that journal would have admired the effort she was making.

The second stirring aspect of Mary's July journal was her reflection on God. From the moment John and I found her in her room that terrible Sunday, I had been brooding over what appeared to be a massive breakdown of faith. If she no longer trusted John or me or the psychiatrist to help her, why hadn't she trusted God? Why had she abandoned hope that God was with her and would sustain her? Of course, those were my questions, not hers, and Mary didn't address them in her journal.

But she did write of her relationship with God. In describing one of her night dreams, she disclosed a surprising mystical sensitivity. "In the dream," she wrote on April 11, 1995, "my mother and I and some other family members were standing in grandma's kitchen. Mom looked into my eyes and said that *she'd* had a dream with Jesus in it. He said to her, 'What if all this religion and theology you've been studying is useless? What if it's *not* as complicated as you think it is? What if I told you I could look in your eyes and warm you from the inside?' God *can* warm me from the inside. It's moments like that which make me remember God is near."

She wrote her friend Kelli a letter in May 1995, while working through her boyfriend breakup: "Thank you for praying for me. You're the only friend I have that I can really talk about God to. God is the only one who can help this situation now, so I'm just praying for everyone and putting my faith in him these days. I hope you'll do the same in your life." My worries about Mary eased a little. God was central to her, it seemed to me, and there was at least a single friend with whom to talk and pray. How could I be anything but thankful for that?

Three weeks before her death, Mary was writing confidently about God: "I think God is the one constant in my life that will endure. People, myself included, are all passing. Everything changes. I look at the effects of religion in my life. When I pray and try to live a Christ-like life, I feel consolation and hope. God is the *one* thing I know I will always have, and I haven't been able to find anything that even comes close to substituting for the Eucharist."

As I read those journal passages, the possibility surfaced that maybe Mary's death had not been a renunciation of God but, rather, a free fall into God's love. Maybe she had staked her life upon that love. There was a moment she and I shared several days before she died, which upon reflection now seemed encouraging. At dinner, I mentioned how we'd discussed Christ as universal savior in Christology class that day. "Father Bowen said, 'If Christ is *not* the universal savior, if Christ wasn't sent to save everyone, I'd rather be driving a bus right now than teaching this class.'" Most students laughed; and when I repeated the remark, I was expecting Mary to laugh. But she only looked at me, and now I sensed why: she was weighing her death in balance with God's saving mercy. She was looking hard before she leaped.

Fortunately, she always wrote the date at the top of her journal entries, so once I finished reading her last notebook, I got the rest of them out of the closet and thumbed through them to find the most recent. I just wanted Mary's point of view, and though it was too late to do anything but weep about it, I wanted to know what had really happened to her. My routine with the journals was to read for a few minutes each day, but after a couple of weeks, I had to stop altogether. The day I ran across her description of the journals as a place of "guilt-free whining," I knew I'd been looking at her through a distorted lens.

Perhaps those people who had cautioned me about reading the journals had been right, because the project ultimately proved frustrating and even agonizing. Although I believed Mary's suffering to be over, her journals were full of dread and confusion, and I couldn't bear to contemplate my daughter ever having suffered at all, especially alone and in silence. And discovering a whimsical turn of phrase every few pages didn't help either. Her wit gave notice to just who and what I had lost.

The suicide note finally arrived from the police station. As was my custom, I was sitting in the living room one October morning with school papers and note cards spread out on the carpet, preparing for my Christology midterm. Studying was a way of imposing order, and I needed order. John walked in looking perturbed. "What's the matter?" I asked.

"I just came back from the police station. I have Mary's suicide note. When the receptionist gave it to me, she looked sick."

I could feel my heart pounding. "What business does she have reading it? Have you read it?"

"Yes."

"And?"

"And I think you need to read it for yourself," he said.

"I plan to."

John handed me the purple notebook he'd been clasping to his chest. *So, this is Mary's final word. This is where I see her honestly, and after this will come nothing more from her ever again.* I cherished and hated the paper upon which she wrote. "I'd rather you not watch me read this."

"I won't watch," John said. "I'll look the other way." So he sat across the room in jacket and tie, with me but looking away from me.

The first thing I saw was "Read Me! A Suicide Note" in large lavender letters on the opening page. Apart from that visible assault, the penmanship appeared normal. Mary began writing in black ink on Saturday, September 23, the day before she died. Her sentences were complete, properly punctuated, and written entirely within the pages' borders, hardly the product of agitation. Beginning with her view of suicide as "darkly mystical," she wrote: "I haven't been silent at all about my suffering, and I doubt anyone is going to be too surprised by my suicide." *You were silent, all right, Mary. And how could you possibly think we wouldn't be surprised?*

"The people who find out are bound to say that they saw this coming anyway," she wrote. "That's assuming they find out at all. The school will probably be reluctant to divulge any of this for fear that others may follow my lead to receive the attention that something like this brings. Those who are saddened will probably say, 'But what could I do? I didn't know her very well.'" Her perception of reality appalled me; I didn't recognize this cynical girl.

Mary attempted to explain what had "driven" her: her nighttime fear of facing school each day, her hope she wouldn't wake up in the morning, her utter aloneness throughout. Although this account of hopelessness was congruent with what she'd revealed in her journals, and therefore familiar, it made me cry in frustration all over again.

But that was not the worst of it. Like the opening "Read me," the second part of the note was written in loopy lavender script and began on "Sept. 24, '95, 12:40 a.m." during the actual pill taking. It started with: "Let the games begin. I've bathed and put on my Sunday best. It's time to celebrate." She continued with a saner couple of paragraphs about loving her friends and family. But then she made an astounding declaration: "Okay. I just finished taking the 2,900 mg of Nortriptyline. In half an hour. I finally had the guts to do *something* decisive."

Oh, my God. She took the pills and kept writing! She could have come and gotten us, and she just kept writing! I wasn't equipped for it. I wasn't prepared to fix my gaze on her opening paragraph that said, in effect, "*Here* I'm alive," and a paragraph two inches farther down that said, "*Here* I'm dying, and I'm glad I'm dying, and there's nothing you can do about it." Reading those words was like watching a slow-motion bullet pierce her skull. I wanted to jump into the page and pull her to safety.

Lauren was in school on the morning I read the suicide note and John Paul was also out of the house, so except for my teary sniffling, the living room was hushed. Looking up from Mary's farewell, I was steadied by white October light dancing on the carpet beside John who, true to his word, was gazing into the distance just beyond me.

"So, now we know," I said. "Wasn't it considerate of her to put the time at the top of the thing so we wouldn't have to guess anymore?"

"She waited until we were asleep," John said. "We would've had to find her in the middle of the night—fat chance. She did it with us sleeping forty feet away. She wanted to show us who was in charge."

"I can't believe she took the pills and just kept writing. I can't; it's too crazy. She doesn't even seem that sad about it."

"I see sadness and lots of anger. I see a disconnect from reality," John said.

"She probably started writing the note on Saturday afternoon. I was vacuuming upstairs and she came up to me and said, 'Mom, are you and Dad going to the monastery tomorrow?' When I told her we were, she smiled and went back to her room. She knew we'd be gone all day Sunday. That's when she probably wrote the first part, before dinner on Saturday. I think that's when she set the thing in motion."

"It's all too much. And I have patients to see at the hospital."

We both stood and hugged each other—two lost parents. He went off to attend patients; I forced myself to keep studying early Christian doctrinal skirmishes. Compared to the suicide note, my classroom notes were downright refreshing. They were rational; I could comprehend them; they gave hope.

Mary's suicide note revealed final hours filled with disordered thinking and a sense of isolation. How awful to realize I could eat with, laugh with, pray with, and talk with my daughter without recognizing her pain—now a deeply mysterious sorrow, which from that moment I would carry for both of us at the center of my heart.

I could have left it alone and tried to get on with my life. I could have put the suicide note in the cardboard box with Mary's journals and shoved it all to the back of my closet, but I wasn't ready. I wasn't ready to let go of the questions that swarmed in my head from morning to night. I was trying to find Mary, and she was somewhere in those questions. Letting go of the questions meant letting go of her. Within a few days, it occurred to me that Mary's psychiatrist might have an answer or two, so I spoke to John about it.

"What if we asked Dr. Matthews to read Mary's note and a few of her journals? Do you think she would?"

"She might. It wouldn't hurt to ask. I'm not sure what she's going to be able to tell us."

"I'm not either, but I bet she could tell us something."

To my surprise, Dr. Matthews agreed to read Mary's notebooks. I arranged them chronologically, numbered them, and took them to her office a few days later with the request that she not make a copy of the suicide note. I still looked upon Mary as a child in need of protection, and I didn't want her words falling into the hands of a medical secretary or physician who had never known her.

John and I finally met with Dr. Matthews on a raw December day. She greeted us pleasantly, but there was apology in her manner. "I set aside an hour," she said, "but we can take all the time we need."

She placed the cardboard box full of Mary's notebooks on the coffee table. Now, though, the notebooks bristled with dozens of red tabs marking significant passages.

"I read the suicide note first," Dr. Matthews said. "I should say I tried to read it. But when I saw, 'So, how do you write yourself out of this world,' I couldn't go any further. It was a couple of days before I was able to pick it back up again. And really, I was never comfortable reading her private journals."

Reading what Mary left behind seemed sensible to me, so I pulled out her final journal, turned to "Read Me! A Suicide Note," and held it up for Dr. Matthews to see.

"I think Mary wanted us to read these things. I could be wrong, but I think that's partly why she wrote them in the first place."

"Well, I had no idea she was writing so extensively," Dr. Matthews said. "The journals were a substitute. . . . If only Mary had told *me* what she was putting in those journals, I might have helped her. I just needed a little more time. When I was at a psychiatric convention last month, I made sure my colleagues heard about her journals. From now on, I ask all my patients whether they keep a journal. They can certainly hide things there."

We were all quiet for a moment. "I don't know for sure," Dr. Matthews said, "but Mary's writings seem to point to borderline personality disorder, maybe not a full-blown case, but nevertheless . . ."

"So," John said, "I guess the arm-cutting incident last winter was part of that."

"Yes. Borderline personality also shows up in extreme anger, relationship difficulties, impulsivity, suicidal tendencies . . . obviously those things are in her journals."

I had heard the term "borderline personality disorder" but knew little about it. "What causes it?" I asked. "Is it some sort of chemical imbalance in the brain?"

"Right now, we're not sure. We think so," Dr. Matthews said.

It was all so vague, and though I wondered what borderline personality disorder bordered *on,* I was not about to ask. Psychiatric answers were no longer worth looking for. They could never bring back Mary who, even if she did show signs of borderline personality disorder, was not *herself* the disorder. Dr. Matthews knew that all along. I think it's why her consultation room was filled with reverence and her comments, every one of them, with sighs. I left tearful and chastened. I hadn't untangled Mary at all. She was mostly beyond my untangling.

Endnotes

20 Anne E. Carr, "Starting with the Human," *A World of Grace,* ed. Leo J. O'Donovan (Washington, DC: Georgetown University Press, 1995), 17.

7

LURCHING FROM *A* TO *B*

Do not go gentle into that good night.
Rage, rage against the dying of the light.
DYLAN THOMAS[21]

ON THE SUNDAY BEFORE COLUMBUS Day in 1995, several of us went to the Big Apple Circus in nearby Reston, Virginia. John's brother Paul and his wife, Linda, had given us tickets the day of the funeral before heading back to Cincinnati.

"You all need some joy in your lives," Linda said. I thanked her even though I knew joy was not riding on those tickets. The mere idea of joy was, in fact, distasteful.

"It's like someone offering you a piece of chocolate cake when you're sick to your stomach," I told John, who didn't disagree.

Just the same, it seemed we owed it to ourselves to push out into the world of color, music, and exuberance. As we were about to leave the house, John Paul said he felt anxious and wanted to stay home, so John stayed with him. But my brother, George, Rita, and their son, Michael, joined me along with Lauren and one of her friends. Once we got seated under the big top, I was able to focus on the red, blue, and green spotlights playing on the stage.

The juggler's gentle performance soothed me, and for a moment I was able to cheer for him. Still, I worried about John Paul at home and Lauren beside me. She seemed more or less all right and certainly not sad, but I kept wondering how, absent a circus, any of us could ever pretend to be happy again. Like a sick person in need of medication, I had to get home and steady myself.

After we ate pizza and returned home, I found John Paul asleep, so I took a walk by myself under an October hunter's moon. Beneath the bright charcoal sky, I saw how "charged with the grandeur of God" the world truly is; and I recalled the last lines of Gerard Manley Hopkins's poem *God's Grandeur*: "Because the Holy Ghost over the bent / World broods with warm breast and with ah! bright wings."[22]

Following close upon that sentiment, however, arrived a complaint: *If you're really brooding over the world, why couldn't you have stopped Mary? Can't you see what we're going through here, and do you care at all?*

I went back home after thirty minutes or so and found John alone in the family room, working on medical charts.

"I've spent the last two weeks trying to see things from Mary's perspective," I said upon walking through the door. "She's the one who took an ax and cut herself off from this family. How dare she look me in the eye knowing I wouldn't see her again? That was cruel."

"I agree," John said. He stood up and walked around the room. "I'm very angry at her. What she did to this family was selfish beyond belief."

We went on that way for a few minutes. How refreshing to say "cruel" for the first time and not be corrected. How nice to look out for myself after spending two weeks leaning over backward for Mary. For fourteen straight days, nearly everything I said had come down to "think how much she suffered." Think how much *she* suffered.

But on the night of the circus, I came to see what had been lurking just below awareness: there were definite *A* issues and *B* issues for me to deal with. So far, the *A*'s had been getting all the attention. Those were the issues having to do with Mary herself. They were the spiritual and psychiatric speculations, the piecing together of her life and death. I had spent nearly every waking moment ruminating about a human and mysterious daughter—a real person, after all—and could still not claim to know who she was or why she did what she did. She had not acted rationally, but irrationally, so the attempt to find logic in her behavior only confounded me.

One thing Professor Martha Manning had said in my foundational theology class the year before helped me recognize this snag: "If you're talking successfully about evil, you're not talking about evil." Because evil actions are irrational, she said, they can't possibly be understood through reason. My daughter's death was evil in view of the damage it had done and would do. It wasn't solvable. It had to be put aside for a time so I could take up the *B* issues that kept worrying me.

The *B*'s focused on family survival, issues concerning how we would endure individually and together. What, for example, was happening to my marriage, the kids, the rest of my family? In view of my numbness, how was I going to be of any use? And how was I supposed to deal with what was going on inside me? Those uncertainties deserved my full concentration, which I tried to give them. But an inner pendulum kept pushing me from *A* to *B*, and from *B* back to *A*; and I couldn't control that movement.

One moment, I would be caught up in the *A*'s and bursting with love, longing and compassion for Mary, and praying to God for her. The next moment, my pendulum would swing back and force attention to my family circumstances. In those moments I would stalk around indignant, feisty, and furious at Mary and praying to God for our survival. I still loved her, and that is the truth, but she had placed herself acutely at odds with me. She and I were estranged, and pouring tears upon Mary alone was jeopardy for me.

Saying, "Mary, I forgive you. Please forgive me" were the required words, so I said them. But considering the emotional wreckage she left behind, mouthing forgiveness meant almost nothing. Real forgiveness, if it was ever to take place, would require much more than words.

Still, I craved the company of people who would sit and listen as I worked through my spaghetti plate of words. It was not something I could expect members of my family to do at any length. Just saying "Mary" in the presence of my mother brought forth an "Oh, God" from her. She was negotiating her own maze of grief not only for Mary but also for my sick father. I could hardly ask her to listen to me. I also got the impression that if my brother and sister weren't saying "Oh, God" it was only because they were trying to be strong for me; and I concluded, probably wrongly, that it was better to leave them alone. My family went into silence about Mary because talking about her was upsetting.

But we stayed close. My neighbor Patricia suggested that some of us women gather for dinner at Olive Garden, one of Mary's favorite restaurants, to honor her on November 13, which would have been her eighteenth birthday. "Mary's birthday can be a day of hiding or a day for honoring her," Patricia said. "The day is coming, one way or another."

So my mother and sister agreed to join Lauren and me at the restaurant. We were accompanied by Patricia and her daughter, as well as a couple of other women close to the family. Mary's best friend Kelli, pale and shaken, came along, too, and sat beside me. Anyone looking our way that night would not have seen the mourning. There was red wine and laughter, even if brittle.

When John asked if we had talked about Mary at the restaurant, I replied, "No, we couldn't even bear to say her name." But I did need to say "Mary." I needed for her not to have fallen off the face of the earth. I had to speak my bewilderment and find some meaning in it.

Hardly anyone, it seems, knew how to take my talkativeness. While Mary's suicide had nothing to do with reason, quite a few people urged me to be reasonable and consider a new perspective on the topic—theirs—seemingly unaware that I'd been turning the subject over in my mind like a lottery drum since her death and had picked through every angle and nuance a thousand times. Most good people ended up offering a philosophy of life's mysteries except for those who were reluctant to say a word for fear of hurting me more.

"Believe me," I told one such person, "nothing you could say about it would hurt my feelings." In fact, peering into Mary's dying face had desensitized me to remarks about my family that normally would have been objectionable.

But it was difficult for people to let me separate my *A* and *B* issues and dig into them. One day over coffee at McDonald's I began with a *B* family issue only to be summarily switched to an *A* Mary issue. "How could Mary betray us like that?" I asked my friend Paula. "How could she sit in her safe little bedroom and . . ." Paula looked up from her coffee, startled.

"Well, she didn't mean to hurt you," she said. "I've heard pain like that can be just awful, especially for a teen. It was probably pure illness."

Paula was only trying to answer my question even though I'd hoped she would see it as rhetorical and not try to answer. She was right in what she said, but her rightness didn't help me. It only made me feel guilty for being angry at Mary and angry at not being heard.

Another time, I began speaking about a Mary issue and was quickly steered to a family issue. After giving my mother a quick version of one of Mary's journal entries and pausing for her comment, I heard this: "How's John doing? I think of him all the time. It must be hard on him, having to get up every day and see patients."

This is not working. No one can stand to listen to me, not even my own mother. Perhaps I shouldn't say these things. My feelings were too raw and unlovely for people, and their attempts to distract me from them irked me even when I knew they were trying to be considerate. A couple of weeks into the grief, a friend who had known Mary since she was a baby invited me to lunch. Only after we'd started eating did Kate tell me she'd hoped we could simply talk in a relaxed way that afternoon. She told me she was thinking that, once reacquainted with each other, we could discuss the suicide another day. Well, even if "another day" was to be the next day, I couldn't wait that long. I had to talk about Mary that day, that hour, that minute.

After his wife died of cancer, Irish author C. S. Lewis kept a journal that he titled *A Grief Observed*. One of the first things he noticed about his bereavement was the "odd by-product" of having become an embarrassment to other people. "At work, at the club, in the street, I see people, as they approach me, trying to make up their minds whether they'll 'say something about it' or not." Even worse, Lewis discovered he'd become a "death's head" to married couples with whom he was acquainted: "Whenever I meet a happily married pair I can feel them both thinking, 'One or other of us must some day be as he is now.'"[23] *Well, at least your wife died honorably of natural causes. My daughter died dishonorably of unnatural causes.*

I perceived myself stranded on a chasm at the edge of a vast space. On my side of the chasm was ruin and abnormality. On the far side was life and normality. It was peopled by those who had never lost someone to suicide and were therefore living happily. I didn't foresee myself ever getting back to the other side, and I couldn't imagine anyone joining me on mine.

Sister Mary Ellen told me one October morning, "You do have to grieve." She was a soul friend with whom I could talk freely, and I trusted her. When John and I entered Carmelite formation six years earlier, we were advised to find a spiritual director, and Sister Mary Ellen had said she would give it a try.

"My husband and I have a good marriage," I was careful to say upon meeting her. "We're not expecting you to do marriage counseling or anything like that."

"That's good," she said with a laugh. During the four years, she had met separately with each of us once a month. At the beginning of the hour, she would place her chair across from mine in the private monastery parlor, whisper a prayer, and ask, "Well, how have you been doing?" She would train her soft blue eyes on me and wait pleasantly. That was the beauty of it; she would wait while I talked.

In the first session, I told her as much as I could about my background and how I'd come to be sitting in her Benedictine parlor. Sister Mary Ellen simply took it all in, asking for clarification a time or two but mostly sitting with her delicate hands folded. Near the end of the hour she said, "Well, God has brought you to this place in your life." It often went that way. All in a rush, I would tell her what had been happening in my life, and she would hear me out. Then she would bring God in.

Sometimes, the topics I brought up were laced with anger, but instead of being put off by the emotion, she encouraged me to keep talking. "But anger makes me unlovable," I said in one of our early sessions.

"No, anger makes you unapproachable," she answered. She let me talk freely about the anger but not carelessly about other people. More than once over the years she told me, "That wasn't a very loving thing to do." Usually, though, she simply commented about God's presence in the current events of my life. In one session some weeks after John Paul fell ill, during his senior year of high school, I was so distressed I could hardly get any words out at all. Apparently at a loss, Sister Mary Ellen finally said, "Well, God loves you." I knew it to be true even though God's love had begun to seem tough and perplexing.

Within a week of Mary's funeral, I found my way to Sister Mary Ellen who, as always, welcomed me to the monastery parlor. She put up the "Room Occupied" sign and then closed the door. *Thank you, God. Here's someone with white hair who knew me when life was sane.* Never having seen her blink at unpleasantness, I began telling her about finding Mary, then the funeral, and how Lauren and John Paul and John were faring. I tried to form words around the topic of how I was doing and ended up blurting, "I don't want people judging me." She said nothing and allowed me to splutter along. But her patience did take the edge off my fear.

"I hope you don't think you're a bad mother."

"How could I not? Anyone who thinks I can just wash my hands of this by saying, 'It's not my fault' doesn't know anything."

She was quiet for a moment and then said, "I wish I had some answers."

"Well, I don't think there are any. Maybe that's a kind of answer right there." She nodded. "But your listening helps a great deal; I appreciate it more than I can say."

Sister Mary Ellen was providing what I most needed: a friend's courage. That's what it took to sit with a newly fashioned "death's head"—courage. Her steadiness began to weave back into place the threads Mary's death had torn. At the end of the hour I said, "So I guess my job is to grieve well."

"Yes, you do have to grieve."

Only years later did Sister Mary Ellen tell me that, as someone who had grieved time and again throughout six decades, she was in awe of the undertaking that lay ahead. She added that suicide grief is much worse than other kinds of grief, but other than telling me to make time each day for myself, she gave no advice. She did not romanticize the situation by telling me I would receive graces from my own saint in heaven. She told me I had to grieve. I had to commit to the reality of Mary's death and find my messy way (she didn't call it messy; that was my label). What she seemed to be urging, though, was a thoroughly human response to the loss of Mary, and I sensed just how messy it was going to be. And even though it sometimes got in the way of conversation, weeping wasn't part of the mess. Weeping was my friend, as I had begun to say, and no one questioned my tears.

In truth, the mother lode of grief was the anger. Friends hinted that I had a right to be angry, and Sister Mary Ellen seemed to think anger was normal. But grieving well meant I had to find out what the anger was all about, to whom I was supposed to be directing it, and how I might keep it from becoming a wrecking ball. It was daunting.

I began writing a journal two days after the funeral. From time to time over the previous dozen years, I had kept a journal of daily life partly to record what was going on with my family, partly to muse, and partly to express feelings. I began writing again for all the usual reasons and one more: to carve wrath into notebook paper where it would lie still.

However, not too many days after talking with Sister Mary Ellen, I began fantasizing about picking up a sledgehammer, going to Mary's bedroom, closing the door, and smashing everything to smithereens: the wooden desk and chair, the chest of drawers, the bedside table, the brass lamp. Of what possible use were those things now that she was gone? Apart from that, why shouldn't I be allowed to address the stupidity, hopelessness, and violence of Mary's death with some stupidity, hopelessness, and violence of my own? It seemed fitting that a roomful of bludgeoned furniture should stand for both our lives, and I assumed people would somehow accept the ruin as a monument to my love. But when it came down to it, I didn't own a sledgehammer, would never have bought one for the purpose, and couldn't bring myself to open Mary's bedroom door for most of a year.

The rage fantasy eventually faded, but the anger didn't go away. It harassed me just as Sister Mary Ellen had warned. "No matter what people say to you," she told me, "you'll find yourself getting angry." And she was right.

One afternoon in the middle of October, John Paul and I sat down to talk. Aside from some minor verbal skirmishes over the previous few days, we had been getting along fairly well. In fact, he'd gone out of his way to greet me with a cheery "Hi, Mom!" whenever I entered the house.

But on that October afternoon when I was feeling particularly guilty for Mary's death, he and I got to talking about her. I should have known better, but I didn't. The moment he hinted that some kind of weirdness in our family might have caused her death, I began yelling at him to get out. John Paul stands more than six feet tall with shoulders like a football lineman, but he scrambled out of the house that day. My neighbor Patricia called a few minutes later to say that he'd come to her house and told her he was afraid he might hurt himself.

"You need to take this seriously," she said. So I called John, and John called Dr. Matthews. She quickly made arrangements to admit John Paul to the psychiatric unit at the hospital.

"John Paul, I'm sorry," I told him. "You didn't do anything wrong. I'm just so angry about Mary . . ."

He might have been projecting his own feeling of weirdness onto the rest of us. But he definitely voiced a trepidation I was trying to fend off: maybe the private inner workings of our family, for which I held myself largely responsible, had contributed to Mary's suicide. Maybe I'd been blind to serious personal flaws that contributed to the disaster. Maybe a grief counselor would eventually probe her way into a shambles at the center of our family.

John Paul told me not to worry about screaming at him, and off he went to the psychiatric unit where he rested for a week and received the new medications, group support, and professional supervision he needed. It was a relief to have him safely out of the house, and he was probably happy to get away from me too. But I was ashamed at having unraveled him with my anger. That simply couldn't happen again. I had to learn to be even-tempered with my son in a way I'd never been before. I could see that his ability to survive depended in large measure on everyday kindness. But the disturbing implications of Mary's death hit me like a punch that October afternoon, and I punched back, unfortunately at the wrong person.

There were other "wrong persons" along the way. One day I reprimanded the newspaper carrier for throwing the evening paper wide of the mark. Another time, I scolded a neighbor for accidentally blowing his autumn leaves into my yard, incidents that normally would have passed without my comment.

One particularly costly encounter took place on a chilly morning after Mass as Father Joe caught up with me in the church courtyard, looked me in the eyes, and asked how I was getting along. As soon as I started to tell him, though, he began looking over my shoulder at some school children several yards behind me. *Forget it. He doesn't care. That's the last time I talk to him.* Regrettably, it *was* the last time I talked to him about Mary before he left All Saints Parish. That my pastor could so readily look away from my grief made me feel foolish. I cut my answer short and hurried away.

Dr. Matthews also began to annoy. Picking up John Paul from an appointment at her office one day, I settled into the waiting room for a few minutes. I thought about how I was probably sitting in a chair Mary had sat in once upon a time. When Dr. Matthews came into the room to say hello, she was cordial, to be sure, but also reserved. *She had a direct responsibility for Mary; but she gets to wake every morning, put on a nice suit, arrange her nice hair, and go through her nicely ordered day. She gets to go on with her life, and I don't.* That's what I was thinking even while I was saying, "Thank-you for everything," and she was responding, "Oh, you're welcome." I said thank-you with a smile, I am sure, because by then I was skilled at putting on a smile and hiding behind it.

Naturally, I was angry with God for the impression I'd gotten my whole church-going life that I'd be rewarded for doing right by my family. I'd thought that delivering, nursing, and staying home with children for more than twenty years was a sacrifice pleasing unto the Lord that would someday blossom forth. On some level of unawareness, I was guided by the idea that hands-on mothering would keep suffering from the door. How stupid of me. Instead of taking beautiful October college tours with Mary, I was now working cemetery trips into my weekly schedule. What should have been a year of special mother-daughter closeness had collapsed into nothingness.

C. S. Lewis observed that while a mother's "God-aimed, eternal spirit" finds comfort in the belief that her deceased child has not lost heaven, she nevertheless has to "write off" the happiness of physical closeness that is "never, in any time or place" to be experienced again.[24] Lewis's observation proved to be true for me. It was the "writing off" of Mary's physical closeness that undid me, especially when I saw old photographs of her.

MARJ AND MARY SWINGING ON AUNT LOUISE'S FARM, 1982.

One favorite photograph showed Mary and me in a swing on my Aunt Louise's farm with sun rays slanting through a scrubby tree in the background. On the June morning of that photograph, I had eased into the swing suspended from a high oak limb while marveling that some things never change. The same swing had hung from the same limb thirty years before when I was five years old.

But on the day of the photograph, it was Mary who was five—a slight, barefoot beauty in white shorts. Testing the rope for sturdiness, I swung higher and higher until, whooping with delight, I slowed to a stop and invited Mary to sit on my lap. When she declined, I said, "C'mon, it'll be okay." Wordless, she sat down and leaned into me, gripping the ropes just above my hands that were clutching hard for both of us. She smiled and looked away from the camera as we swept into the warm air. I smiled, too, because on that sweet Georgia morning in 1982, she was holding her slim, precious body next to mine. That she would never do so again in any time or place was a fact I was going to have to accept.

One rule I was learning to ignore originated in childhood. It was: "Don't say bad things about the dead" because "they're not here to defend themselves." I obeyed the rule throughout life and refrained from speaking ill of the dead who could not defend themselves. But now I needed to say bad things about the dead, or at least true things that happened to be bad. Tiptoeing around Mary only resulted in sniping at the wrong people.

In *Silent Grief: Living in the Wake of Suicide*, Christopher Lukas and Henry Seiden give three reasons for suicide survivor rage: being rejected by someone who did not consider the survivor "important enough" to remain living for; being abandoned by someone the survivor loved; and being accused as though the dead person were "pointing a finger and saying, 'You didn't do enough for me.'"[25] From the beginning, rejection, abandonment, and accusation swam inside me like sharks; but it was the last one, the implicit finger pointing, that made me the angriest.

It took several months, but I finally confronted that anger. Standing alone on the slope of Mary's grave one wintry afternoon, I started to kneel but instead stood upright and shouted my own accusations onto the granite headstone. I accused my daughter of unbelievable violence and of giving up on me, who could have helped. Only after I'd said every angry thing I could think of did a sliver of peace take hold within. How invigorating to find my voice and rain down anger on Mary where it belonged. Afterward, I had to tell myself daily that it was she who took the pills, that I didn't make her take them, and that it was she who was presumably at peace while I was straining to make it through the day.

The sting of rejection, abandonment, and accusation endured, just the same, and when I thought about Mary's death (I missed her the way I would have missed a severed hand), the words "deeply offensive" rolled through me. Family members accepted my use of the phrase, I think without quite agreeing on its aptness. What was so offensive about the death of a sick daughter that I couldn't get beyond? Early on in the grief, I said, while weeping, to Sister Mary Ellen, "I knew there was a bond, of course, but I never knew it was this deep." Why, though, was the wrenching of that bond so thoroughly insulting?

One clue finally appeared in the comment of a Christian Brother during one of my classes. "With men," Brian said, "love of God isn't a matter of words; it's the willingness to shed blood. Shedding blood shows you really mean it." But as a woman, I had shed blood for God by shedding it for Mary; and I had really meant it. In the moment before she swallowed that first Nortriptyline pill, why had the shedding of my blood counted for nothing with my daughter?

I knew my relationship with John Paul was always different from the one I had with Mary. While I was elated to find myself several weeks pregnant with him and considered him from the start my new little companion, I was more focused on the strange expansion of my body than I was on him. I went to the doctor on schedule, took vitamins, and paid attention as was my obligation, but I didn't intentionally enter into the unfolding inner mystery of John Paul. I didn't know how.

After nine months of unprecedented internal goings-on and one unnerving night of labor—of odd abdominal pressures, of bearing up and bearing down—when at dawn John Paul's slithery gray body surged forth in blood, all I could say was, "Well, I'll be damned." In the joy of that instant, no one was paying attention to my words. Yet, even as the obstetrician was suturing me back together, I knew how completely I had been thrust into the royal sorority of motherhood, how completely unready for it I was, and how vital it was for me to enter into its significance then and there.

Because of John Paul, I was able to watch for Mary three years later, sensing her existence even before the telling absence of menstrual blood. As soon as it made sense medically to do so, John drew my blood to see whether it contained the hormone hCG (human chorionic gonadotropin), signaling the formation of a placenta. "Your blood test came back," he told me, with a smile, "and it was positive!"

When I later went to the bookstore searching for a pregnancy medical guide, what caught my eye was a book of intrauterine color photographs titled *A Child Is Born: The Drama of Life before Birth*. I was captivated. One page consisted entirely of the enlarged photograph of an embryo at twenty-eight days gestation, a sixth of an inch long, floating at the end of the umbilicus. The embryo was translucent pink with the tinge of blood and resembled a tiny cocktail shrimp. *This is how my baby looks right now! And in two more weeks, her arms, legs, body, and face will take shape just as the book describes: "as though sculptured from inside."* [26]It was God forming Mary's inmost being and knitting her in the darkness of my womb.

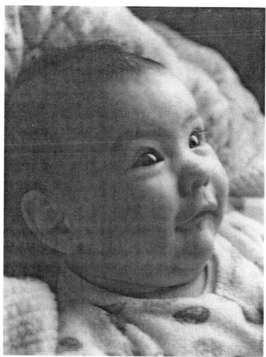

MARY AT FOUR MONTHS OF AGE, 1978.

Six months into a pregnancy that felt in the first weeks like a delicious secret, there was blood one hot August morning; it was only a few drops but impossible to ignore after John told me there should be no blood whatsoever. At his urging, I went to the obstetrician who examined me and then instructed me to go home to bed. Dr. Roberts assured me that getting off my feet was the best thing I could do and that the spotting might disappear on its own. Was that all he could advise? Get off my feet? His remedy seemed feeble over against the prickly fear of miscarriage rising inside.

I left the doctor's office in tears and ventured down the street to John's office. "Whatever comes," he said with a long hug, "we'll face it together."

Seeing the worry in his eyes added a measure of dread; did he know something I didn't know? So I did the only thing I could do: I went home to bed. I probably prayed with the same two words I used for Mary in the emergency waiting room eighteen years later: *please . . . heal.* In a day or two, the spotting stopped and did not recur. But the incident impressed upon me the fragile blood link I shared with my daughter.

In reflecting upon that link, I included the moment two days after Mary's birth that a nurse came into my hospital room to draw blood from me. Propped in bed, I was holding my newborn girl who was doing one of the few things she knew how to do: breast-feed. And I was doing one of the few things I knew how to do: gaze at her. It was symbiotic. Mary needed the nourishment, and even though her sucking made me wince at first with discomfort, I needed her to empty the rapidly filling breast milk.

Just as the nurse was finishing the blood draw, she accidentally squirted two drops onto my nightgown—bold red on mint green—that washed out of the garment but lingered in my mind as a sign of the donation I had made, would continue to make, and was rightly expected to make for Mary. That she could brush it aside while writing her suicide note was a persistent outrage.

However, the blood tie doesn't get underneath all the anger I was trying to uncover. There was also a long smudge of resentment over Mary's rejection of her God-given miraculous being. To clarify: my father was a backyard gardener who plowed long and deep. On spring Saturdays as a child, I would look out the window and see him striding behind his plow, dividing soil into furrows for holding seeds and bearing summer fruit. But in the sharp winds of April, the plowing was hard, muddy work and not something I wanted to help with or even watch. A day came, though, that my father called me out back to see something.

"Look what I found," he said, wiping dirt off a gray stone. "It was way down beneath the surface. Probably hasn't seen the light of day for a *thousand years.*"

Taking it in hand, I could see it was more than an ordinary rock. It was a rock wonderful and worthy of respect, not unlike a treasure buried in a field, which as I would hear much later was something like the kingdom of heaven.

Mary was just such a wonder to me, my own special wonder: a daughter, a mother, a sister, and a friend. She was cartwheel and poetry, a treasure for which, out of joy, I went and sold all I had. Then she was gone.

MARY AND MARJ, 1978.

Endnotes

21 Dylan Thomas, "Do Not Go Gentle into That Good Night," *Literature: An Introduction to Fiction, Poetry, and Drama*, compiled by X. J. Kennedy (New York: Harper Collins Publishers, 1991), 675.

22 Gerard Manley Hopkins, "God's Grandeur," *Hopkins: Poems and Prose* (New York: Alfred A. Knopf, 1995), 14.

23 C. S. Lewis, *A Grief Observed* (New York: Bantam Books, 1976), 10, 11.

24 Ibid., 30.

25 Christopher Lukas and Henry M. Seiden, *Silent Grief: Living in the Wake of Suicide* (Northvale, NJ: Jason Aronson Inc., 1997), 56.

26 Axel Ingelman-Sundberg and Claes Wirsen, *A Child Is Born: The Drama of Life Before Birth* (New York: Dell Publishing Co., 1965), 59.

8

CLAIMING FAMILY

We are preserved in love by the goodness of God
just as truly in woe as in well-being.
JULIAN OF NORWICH[27]

AFTER JOHN PAUL CAME HOME from the hospital psychiatric unit in late October, I realized we were a family on edge. It wasn't something I could talk about, but I woke each day in fear for my husband, my children, and myself. Part of that fear, I now know, was simply grief, a connection C. S. Lewis noted in the first line of *A Grief Observed*: "No one ever told me that grief felt so like fear."[28] I was undergoing the "fluttering in the stomach" Lewis describes along with the restlessness, the yawning, and the swallowing: all normal grief reactions. But I was also experiencing a kind of fright that had little to do with normal grief and everything to do with the guilt, blame, and mistrust that go along with suicide.

"It's as though our family has been blown apart from inside," I told a friend, "and that makes it much worse."

John and I knew we had to pull ourselves together, close ranks, and stabilize our family.

It took no time for an advantage to emerge out of what had seemed a disaster: John Paul's schizoaffective disorder. Over the previous three years, his illness had taught us respect for the delicacy of brain chemistry. From the start, John and I were less inclined to blame ourselves for Mary's death, which we had every reason to think resulted from faulty brain chemistry.

"In a way, John Paul prepared us for what happened with Mary," I told a few people who, looking vaguely surprised, did grant the possibility of some benefit. That John and I were less inclined to blame ourselves for Mary does not mean we refrained from it altogether, only that we had a running start toward truth.

A second advantage to our family was that John and I were friends. We had operated as a married team for more than twenty years and counted on each other. He left the house between 7:00 and 8:00 each weekday morning, saw his last office patient around 5 p.m., and then made hospital rounds for a couple of hours. But he still managed to come through the door at night with a smile, and I liked that about him.

After dinner, he and I sat at the table and talked. Over time, those few minutes cemented something vital in my adult formation. It wasn't as though there was no grousing about the day's frustrations in the form of broken toilet handles or broken patient appointments—there was plenty of that. It was that John spoke respectfully of the sick people he tried to help, especially those at life's end for whom he could offer nothing but his presence.

"I stopped by the intensive care unit this morning to see a patient whose kidneys are shutting down," he said once or a dozen times. "The family was by the bedside and wanted to pray, so we did."

He was regularly bringing to the dinner table stories of people who were teetering on the doorstep of death, not to sort through their medical problems but to acknowledge a small part of their humanity. "One of my patients with Alzheimer's no longer recognizes anybody," he would tell me. "But she can still pick up on a tone of voice, so we have to be careful how we speak around her."

In early marriage, I listened to those end-of-life narratives more out of obligation than interest. Only after years of sitting with John did I come to value the human dignity and vulnerability he was setting on the table each evening. It was a glance at fundamental reality, a privilege, I would not have been granted except for John.

At the table, I would relate snippets about the children. "Lauren says she wants to play drums next year in the school band"; "John Paul got an A on the biology quiz he was worried about"; "Do you think it'd be okay for Mary to go to Virginia Beach this weekend with Susan's family?" What I had to say about the kids was nice and easy. "I don't think I've ever lost a night's sleep worrying about the kids," I offered one night.

"We'll have our trials just like everybody else," John answered.

After Mary died, our conversations were no longer nice and easy. There was weeping, indignation, and glassy-eyed bafflement. We agreed that our intention to protect the children, moreover every good thing we had tried to do, had been trampled upon. That evaluation happened not to be true, but it felt true, and that made it worth saying. It helped to know we could eat breakfast together the next morning without being held to account for what we said the evening before.

I had heard that a high percentage of marriages end in divorce following the death of a child. It was a distressing thought but also increasingly beside the point. As time went on, John and I seemed to be drawing closer.

"He's a good Catholic," my mother said after John asked me in 1971 to marry him. "He won't be thinking about divorce down the road." Southern Methodist that she was, she had upheld matrimony as staunchly as any Catholic. "Marriage is sacred," she would tell me, and observing the life she and my father shared, I could believe her.

Theologians of the Second Vatican Council wrote that a married woman and man "become conscious of their unity and experience it more deeply from day to day." [29] I was indeed conscious of unity with John, and I think he was conscious of unity with me. It was a unity of great sadness after Mary's death, but it was unity just the same.

What concerned me during that time of mourning was not so much our marriage. It was the sorrow weighing on John Paul and Lauren who couldn't talk about what they were going through. Not having endured the death of a sister, I couldn't comprehend their anguish, but I saw the effect of it. When John Paul tried to chat with Lauren in the afternoon about school, for instance, she would scowl and yell, "Leave!" He would leave, but not without complaining sharply.

The way they were acting toward each other, while not surprising, nevertheless chilled me. I kept thinking of Mary's place in their lives. She had held the middle ground as a buffer, and now they were forced to bridge a ten-year age gap and relate directly. It would just take time, I told myself, while suspecting that the real predicament was something bleaker: neither of them could *be* Mary for the other. Unable to remedy the situation, I wanted more than anything to run from it.

MARY AND LAUREN, 1989.

It was not the first time I'd wanted to run from the kids. I'd also felt that impulse during a beach vacation in 1978. John Paul was four years old at the time and Mary was a baby. One late afternoon, John and I decided to walk down the beach with the kids on the hard-packed sand after the July heat had fallen off a little. The radiant sky under which we started our walk quickly turned to slate; and we found ourselves alone on a wide expanse of blowing sand, turning for home just as thunder rolled in. Having once heard of someone killed by lightning on a beach, I wanted nothing more than to leave everyone behind and take off running.

I picked up John Paul and helped John steer Mary's stroller toward the nearest beach path. We made it home soaked, but I couldn't dismiss either the speed with which danger had sprung upon our family or my selfish inclination to run. Bringing children into the world meant I owed them protection at all costs. That's what the beach episode showed.

Now, though, I found myself wanting to run both from the gloom of my family and the gloom within me. Poet Gerard Manley Hopkins wrote: "I wake and feel the fell of dark, not day."[30] It was an accurate description of my daily waking. Even before my eyes opened, interior darkness seeped through me, and within half a second came the startling, "Oh God, she's really gone." I understood the anesthesia of early grief to be wearing off and the slog through days, weeks, and years without Mary to be commencing in full. I understood that the psychological denial that had been my companion was now fading.

Once or twice, I thought about packing a suitcase, signing Lauren out of school, loading her into the brown Custom Cruiser station wagon, and driving into the sunset. I thought Lauren and I might relax in a motel room for a few days and watch kids' movies in bed. We would then go home, and life would be easier. John and everyone else would understand that I had not intended to leave them but just to draw breath someplace out of the reach of sadness. However, it was only a mind game. I couldn't run from reality no matter how far I went.

"If someone gave me a million dollars and told me to vacation in Italy for six months," I said, "it wouldn't do any good. The grief would go to Italy with me." There was no escaping the darkness; I was bound to it, and it was bound to me.

Yet, the darkness was revealing itself as not entirely dreadful. It had about it a sense of obscurity and unknowing: a sense, in other words, that God was working even if I didn't know how. Having gone through such darkness at the onset of John Paul's illness, I had felt its friendliness. In 1992 just after my son's mental health had begun to improve, I was asked to give a short talk about my experience of secular Carmelite life.

"The son I thought I knew was slipping away from me," I told my community, "and I could not be sure I would ever get him back. It felt at times as though plates and cups were being smashed inside me."

Then I told of moments during his illness that had registered upon me as sacred. "When John Paul and I were alone in the house and could sit at the kitchen table and talk, it was clear God wanted me to love my son just as he was at that moment. No matter how mysterious or painful life might be, God is in the darkness, drawing near in love." It was a perspective I had gained from John of the Cross who was always teaching me, it seemed, to name God in the night.

The perception of light-in-darkness gave me hope after Mary died. More and more compelling was God's tenderness, which after years of reading about it in the Canticle of Zechariah at Morning Prayer, I started to see anew, given the straits of my family. Zechariah proclaims the tender compassion of God by which the dawn from on high breaks upon us, shines on those who dwell in darkness and the shadow of death, and guides their feet into the way of peace. I gradually perceived divine compassion shining through the shadow of death that lay over my family, and I was strengthened each day to the point of wanting to stand firm and not run.

Being guided into the way of peace meant, for one thing, that everyone in the family had to try to receive what was then being offered: grief therapy. Our first therapy appointment was scheduled for Halloween afternoon, so Lauren would have to cut short her after-school party planning and go immediately with John Paul and me to a hospital consultation room. John Paul who had only just been discharged from the hospital would have to trust that going back for additional therapy might not be a waste of time. Over in his office, John would have to remove his stethoscope and hurry across the street to join us. I felt that it was up to me to show a little optimism.

We had arranged to meet that Halloween day with a clinical social worker that Dr. Matthews had recommended. "Hi there," Jane said with a smile. "Why don't y'all come into my office?"

We filed into the cramped room. It was the moment of scrutiny I had feared since the day of Mary's death five weeks earlier. I thought I'd better take a seat beside John lest Jane think he and I were out of sorts. On the other hand, how would it look if I chose not to sit beside my son or daughter? Having worked with John Paul in the psychiatric unit, Jane already knew something of the inner workings of our family. I was leery of her. Maybe she'd be able to see through pretense; maybe she'd see my contribution to the trouble we were in.

But she also had to know something about the steadiness of our family. Two weeks earlier when John Paul was in the psychiatric unit, Jane had interviewed John and me. "Aside from

Mary," she asked, "has anyone in the family died?" She went on to inquire whether we had moved recently, whether John Paul had changed schools often as a boy, and whether he had suffered from chronic illness when he was young. The answer was "no" to those and all other questions that were designed to uncover family strain. The questionnaire ended up making us look like a stable, if not downright fortunate, family. I hoped that Jane would recognize the puzzle pieces I'd been trying to fit in place; because as far as I could understand, no family event or pattern of events could be said to have triggered John Paul's illness or Mary's suicide. Yet, there we were at Halloween, all haunted and huddled together.

As a high-school student, I never spent time in a principal's office; but I doubt the indignity would have made me want to stand up and shout, "No fair!" any more than my first minute on Jane's loveseat. Clearly, she was in charge and I was not. It was her job to break through our defenses and lead us into reality. She began by telling us how good it was to see us all. She asked if we could give her some idea of what we hoped to gain through family therapy.

"We just need to come together," I said, "and get things out in the open."

"Right," John said. "We need some kind of openness. I've dealt with suicidal patients, but I never thought my daughter was suicidal."

Jane expressed sympathy for Mary's death, for its aftermath, and for our having to sit in her office where she knew we would rather not be sitting.

We agreed that improved family communication was a good place to start. Who would've questioned such common sense? Better talking and listening was a worthy goal even if a purported failure to talk and listen had not, in my opinion, ever been at the heart of our troubles. As far as I was concerned, our recovery as a family hinged on something more than improved communication skills, perhaps something as simple and difficult as sitting together in a room for twenty-five Thursday afternoons and recommitting our wounded selves to each other.

Given the chance to talk about their grief that first day, both John Paul and Lauren hesitated. Lauren talked about life in the sixth grade and then said, "After school, sometimes I ride my bike with Cindy and Beth." She jiggled her running shoe and smiled, obviously relieved that Jane wasn't trying to get her to say more.

Asked how he had been getting along, John Paul leaned forward, elbows on knees, and looked at the floor. "I feel a *lot* better." His attempt to be upbeat for the sake of our family showed a generous spirit and gave me, at least, a touch of relief.

"I hear you've been taking your medications every day," Jane said. "Good! What about your daily plan?" John Paul had withdrawn from George Mason University and was too ill at ease even to look for a job. But Jane had tried during his hospital stay to have him write down small daily goals.

"I *try* to write down a plan each day," he said. "I *try* to keep organized. Geez, it's hard to do around our house."

He had been spending a good part of each day in his bedroom listening to music and pacing. He and I talked at different points, but being without his sister was a lonesome place to be. For seventeen of his twenty-one years, Mary had been a fine sister and friend. John Paul looked up to her. As a young teen, he once accidentally knocked over her science project in the basement, breaking several plant stalks and pretty much ruining six weeks of work.

"What are you going to do now?" I asked him.

"The first thing I do is tell Mary."

Seeing him grieve for her reduced me to deep breaths and leaps of faith. They were not exactly big leaps; they were tiny steps or perhaps nothing more than a holding of ground, because everything I did seemed ineffectual. I couldn't patch up my son's hurt; I had to believe him when he said he would never do what Mary did. I couldn't make it through the day otherwise. Mary had already thrown ice water on my illusion of control, so how could I think—really, deep down—that I might control John Paul? What I had to do was give up the notion of being in charge of his life, while at the same time supporting the daily structure our therapist was trying to help him work out.

"Well, John Paul," Jane said, "we'll just have to keep at it until we come across some things you might want to do with your day. Okay? But you can't just be hanging out all the time."

"Sure," he replied.

I thought he'd probably continue to hang out but didn't say so. Relinquishing for a moment my role as family spokesperson, I draped my arm over the back of the loveseat and tried to look unworried.

At the end of that first hour, we decided to meet the next Thursday afternoon at 4:00 and kept on meeting until we had completed six months of Thursday afternoons. I won't say the sessions relieved sadness—they usually stirred it—or that their dollar cost was ever far from my mind. John had to leave a big opening in his Thursday patient schedule in order to be with us, and occasionally one of us had to be somewhere other than Jane's office.

Naturally, there was some griping. Lauren told me she thought the whole thing was dumb and boring. Maybe that was the only description she could come up with. In *The Grieving Child,* Helen Fitzgerald writes that children often act out in anger when someone dies because they lack the capacity to understand or articulate what is happening.[31] For the most part, Lauren didn't act out. She went to school every day, did her homework, and seemed to enjoy sleepovers with her girlfriends.

Not only that but she also joined the All Saints sixth-grade girls basketball team and played rugged defense, eventually winning the Most Spirited Award at the end of the season. For Christmas that year, we gave her a set of drums, which she played in the basement every afternoon. I always thought running off sadness on the basketball court and pounding it out on drums were good substitutes for the words she couldn't speak.

During those months of therapy, in fact, Jane tried to lead us all out of the fog and get us to talk about our hurt, anger, and bewilderment. It proved more than a little challenging. During one sluggish session several weeks into the therapy, she said, "Suicide is the ultimate angry thing to do. Y'all are being too nice about it. What happened in your home was abnormal. It was murder."

No one said anything, and no one flinched. Murder? Looking around, I saw empty stares.

"Never really thought of it that way," I said. The room remained quiet and the subject was dropped.

Still, Jane kept trying to pry our feelings loose. She once suggested that John and I go home, sit down, and have a good argument.

But after a few weeks without argument, I ended up telling her, "No matter what John did or didn't do for Mary, I wouldn't have done any better. I *didn't* do any better. We're kind of fragile, so I don't think arguing will help."

"It's good you respect each other's vulnerability," she replied, "but at some point, you might find that you're angry with each other."

With that, John revealed that sometimes he got mad at himself and sometimes at me. His admission didn't upset me; I was glad to hear it. After Mary had treated us so dishonestly, honesty had risen to the top of my list of virtues. More than ever, I prized candor and found myself mentally dismissing people who I suspected were not being open with me. So I considered John's anger minor compared to the big surf we'd been thrown into and were surviving together.

In February, Jane asked John and me to come alone for a session the following week. As soon as we settled on her loveseat and offered pleasantries, she asked the question I thought she was going to ask: "How's your sex life?"

"Depressed," I said, as John nodded. "But then, so are a lot of other things like shopping. Just today, I went shopping and *hated* it." I also hated that Jane had brought sex into it, as though that could possibly be a gauge of suicide healing.

"Try to think of sexual intimacy as a comfort for now," she advised.

"Okay," we both said.

I might have added we'd been hit on the head by a two-by-four and were numb to everybody, including each other. I would have added it if only I'd come to terms with the staying power of my own shock. I knew Mary's death was traumatic, but I wasn't yet aware that the trauma had given rise to a form of Post-traumatic Stress Disorder.

In their work on suicide survivorship called *Silent Grief,* Christopher Lukas and Henry Seiden make the case for Post-traumatic Stress Disorder.[32] They write of suicide survivors who commonly experience a flattening of their feelings and a detachment from other people. During the months of family therapy and for many months afterward, I was encased emotionally in cotton. I wondered if I'd ever again relate to people with normal give-and-take.

What I needed throughout that period was mildness in all its forms: no arguments or loud voices, no strife or contention. I wanted to sit quietly by myself, preferably in the sunshine on the patio, and study. I wanted to watch brown leaves fall off oaks. I wanted music that did not excite, and I wanted a favorite recording of Gregorian chant playing at night in the bedroom before John and I went to sleep. I wanted to hold his hand in the dark. It was the best I could do, but there was no way of telling Jane that.

Her attempts to get our feelings out in the open did succeed here and there, even though it seemed that none of us was ready for deep disclosure. Only in 1998 at the Union while sitting in a class called Death and Pastoral Care of the Dying did I begin to understand my family's reticence during therapy. From the first day of class, it was obvious that priests, seminarians, religious sisters, and lay students were there not only to learn about bereavement ministry but also to work through personal grief.

"For every one of you sitting here today," said Elizabeth, the professor, "I could go out in the halls and find twenty-five other people who are grieving. Grief is widespread; almost everybody is grieving some kind of loss."

That was strangely encouraging. So in introducing myself, I told the class what had happened to Mary. I stopped short of telling what had happened to me.

The most helpful part of the class was its emphasis on the grief process. Elizabeth gave us a chart called The Process of

Grieving, which depicted several common bereavement traits holding true across cultures: shock and denial, pain and work, emptiness, and finally, perhaps resolution. Grief resolution, she explained, entails making a new place for the deceased person in your emotional life so that you can get on with your own life. Resolution requires honoring both the dead and the living. Elizabeth told us that grief resolution often requires years, involves real effort, and may not always take place.

You have to try to heal. That was the lesson of my class about death. A great deal, it was said, depended on not getting stuck in denial, anger, guilt, or depression, and thus becoming incapable of making peace and moving on. Happily, the grief chart Elizabeth handed me was lightweight; it contained the rough outlines of bereavement on a single sheet of paper. Maybe with effort over time, my family's grief would run its course from shock and pain to resolution. Maybe God would finally bring it to an end as clean as the paper's edge.

That simple grief chart made me realize that my family had been abiding in shock and denial throughout those six months of therapy. Each of us, in fact, seemed lodged in disbelief. A passage in Lewis Carroll's *Through the Looking Glass* speaks to the situation. When Alice protests that "one *can't* believe impossible things," the Queen tells her she probably hasn't practiced enough and that she herself, through daily practice, has sometimes believed "as many as six impossible things before breakfast."[33]

For me, Mary's death was an impossible thing arriving each day before breakfast. Believing it took hundreds of days of practice—morning, noon, and night—and would not be rushed. Sister Mary Ellen put it to me this way: "Of course you're not going to get over a shock like that in six months." Along with the daily practice of believing my daughter's suicide came the need for patience, patience, patience.

Jane gave practical advice about surviving suicide. During one session she addressed a misperception more deep-rooted than the "what if" questions John and I had been asking ourselves, such as: What if we had sent Mary to a different psychiatrist? What if we had tried to peek into her bedroom that Sunday morning? What if I had sprained an ankle when I fell in the street the day before she died and stayed home from the monastery that Sunday? Those were questions without answers, crazy-making questions that would finally have to end. The misperception calling for the most clarity, however, concerned human limitations. In that touchy area, Jane did her best work.

"We were out of it where Mary was concerned," John once told Jane. "We should have been playing defense, and we were standing on the sideline."

"That's for sure," I said. "If only I'd read one of those journals. A couple of weeks before Mary died, I overheard a woman talking about her high-school daughter. She said something like, 'That girl is always on the run. She's so involved, I hardly ever see her anymore.' The woman was clearly delighted with her daughter. It drove home what I was feeling for Mary, and it wasn't delight. It was more like fear. I was scared for her without knowing why."

"Okay, here are some things to think about," Jane said. "In the first place, you weren't wrong about those journals. I imagine you were just trying to create some trust with your daughter. Give yourself some credit for that. Second, I think your daughter brought deficits into the family which y'all couldn't overcome."

"What do you mean?" John asked.

"It sounds like Mary was romanticizing death. Teens will do that. They can't imagine what death means. And Mary obviously couldn't take in anything positive about herself. I tell my depressed patients they have their filters on backward. They filter out all the positive things in their lives and keep the negative. Teens sometimes look inside themselves and get so frightened they can't tell you what's going on. Those are huge deficits for you two to deal with."

With that my grief became slightly more manageable.

"After all, you're not decoders or mind readers," Jane said. "If Mary couldn't let you know what was going on, how were you supposed to help her? As parents, you're just not that powerful."

"You're just not that powerful." All along, I thought I was that powerful. Even after John Paul's mental illness revealed my lack of sway in the large events of life, I continued to count on maternal instinct for power. I continued to dine upon the rich regard for maternal with-it-ness flowing from Mother's Day homilies and papal pronouncements of the kind Pope John Paul II made in 1988.

"It is commonly thought that women are more capable than men of paying attention to another person," he wrote in *On the Vocation and Dignity of Women*, "and that motherhood develops this predisposition even more."[34] But even if completely true, that statement doesn't address the difference between paying attention and knowing. I paid attention to Mary (or thought I was paying attention) without knowing her when she needed to be known.

"You're just not that powerful." Of all the remarks aimed my way those early grieving months, that one was most incisive. It allowed me to come down off my perch of motherly knowing and reckon with my human shortfall. Even more, it suggested a path through two extreme thoughts. The first extreme was this: I am responsible for Mary's death. Almost always, that was quickly replaced by: I can't be answerable for what took place behind her locked door. But even so, a sickening variation cropped up from time to time: I let her die. She was trying to tell me how alone she felt, and I refused to hear it.

I would push that reproach away and shift to the other extreme: Nothing I ever said or did could possibly have led to such an outcome. That was the more tenable position except for this: If nothing I said or did could have led to such an outcome, what about the fact that I was her mother and among the last to see her? What about my sense of personal fiasco while standing at her grave several dozen times with the words "This is so wrong" knifing through me?

Mary had her deficits and I had mine. How responsibility for her death might be parceled out, I couldn't say. Maybe it was better to use "You're just not that powerful" as a mantra for a while, surrender everything to God, stop searching for answers, and find a way to live with the ambiguity.

In mid-May, my family sat on Jane's loveseats for the final time. It felt like graduation. I was encouraged that we had banded together as a family but reluctant to end our relationship with Jane. She looked around, smiled, and commended us for having attended each week. She said our taking on the demanding work of suicide grief indicated we would be able to handle difficult situations in the future. "If you can deal with this," she said, "you can deal with anything."

She said she didn't doubt we'd heal but that her door would remain open. Her comments were an official notice of goodness and a benediction. Moved to tears I didn't want Jane to see, I hurried out of her office with the excuse that I needed to get home and fix dinner.

But after thinking about her contribution, I did thank Jane in a note: "Each of us has fallen to the earth like grains of wheat and died, but your presence to our dying has been a kind of rebirth." That was it: her presence to our dying.

JOHN PAUL, LAUREN, MARJ, AND JOHN AT THANKSGIVING, 1998.

A month later, John Paul went back to George Mason University for summer classes and earned A's in child psychology and computer basics. John began figuring out how to merge his medical practice with that of another internist in town. For fun, we all visited The Flying Circus Airshow in a nearby town one June Sunday and watched skydiving and wing-walking. On another Sunday, we floated on inner tubes down the warm Potomac River.

And Lauren and I finally took the getaway trip I'd fantasized about. Instead of traveling in the brown Custom Cruiser and sleeping in a motel, we rented a red Thunderbird and drove across the Allegheny Mountains to Ohio. There, we visited Theresa, an 85-year-old family friend who had always stashed candy in a "magic drawer" for the kids, cooked pasta dinners from scratch, and who, far from being intimidated by our grief, embraced it as though she had spent her whole life preparing for it.

Endnotes

27 Julian of Norwich, *Showings*, ed. Richard J. Payne (Mahwah, NJ: Paulist Press, 1977), 176.

28 C. S. Lewis, *A Grief Observed*, 1.

29 "Church in the Modern World," in *Vatican Council II: The Conciliar and Post Conciliar Documents*, ed. Austin Flannery, O.P., (Collegeville, MN: The Liturgical Press, 1987), 950.

30 Gerard Manley Hopkins, "I Wake and Feel," *Hopkins: Poems and Prose* (New York: Alfred A. Knopf, 1995), 71.

31 Helen Fitzgerald, *The Grieving Child: A Parent's Guide* (New York: Simon & Schuster, 1992) 114.

32 Christopher Lukas and Henry M. Seiden, *Silent Grief*, 28.

33 Lewis Carroll, Martin Gardner, and John Tenniel, *The Annotated Alice: The Definitive Edition* (New York: W.W. Norton & Company, 1999), 199.

34 Pope John Paul II, *Mulieris Dignitatem*. 1988, 22. http://www.vatican.va/holy_father/john_paul_ii/apost_letters/documents/hf_jp-ii_apl_1508

9

SEARCHING

The Soul selects her own Society --
Then -- shuts the Door –
EMILY DICKINSON[35]

MARY CAME TO ME IN nighttime dreams for a couple of years following her death. She seemed self-confident and very much in charge of our few seconds together. I sensed she had the power to evaporate before my eyes, so I whispered to keep her near. Keeping her near was everything; her dream presence made me feel whole again. On a January night in 1997, however, I experienced her spirit in a new way.

"Last night," I told Sister Mary Ellen, "I dreamed I was trying on clothes at Fair Oaks Mall, and I was wearing Mary's gold earrings, which I always wear." Sister focused her gaze on me. "When I realized I'd lost one of the earrings, I told the saleslady I had to go find something and began wandering around the mall looking for it. First, I found two pearl earrings on the floor and then turned around and found the gold one."

Quiet for a few seconds, Sister Mary Ellen finally said, "I believe dreams are a way God speaks to you. What do you think about all this?"

"Well, the first part is about trying on things. That would be me going back to school. It's also about losing Mary and feeling frantic. I dropped everything to go look for that earring. Lots of people were walking by, and I was surprised someone else didn't see it first. Mary left me gold—*she's* the gold. And in looking for her, I found the pearls."

"What are they?"

"Maybe they have something to do with the pearl of great price. Maybe there's something mystical between Mary and me. Maybe it's about searching for her and finding God."

"You've been searching all along," Sister said, and that was true.

The August after finishing family therapy in 1996, John and I traveled to Charleston, South Carolina, for a doctors' seminar on hypertension. We needed to get away and the weekend was pleasant, even if filled with sadness at moments. While John was in class one morning, I left the hotel and visited a nearby open-air market, which was packed with sea-shell crafts, bright baskets, watercolors, and dozens of pretty hand-stitched goods. I found myself bored and restless while walking through the displays, looking and not looking. After a few minutes in the steamy air, I realized that nothing in the market would ever satisfy and walked back lonely and empty-handed to the hotel. All along, it was Mary's face I had been searching for in the crowd.

That was one kind of searching, the simple kind, and it didn't go on for more than a year. But another kind of search was going on all the time: the search for a way to get Mary back in my life. That was what I wanted—Mary back in my life—but in a real way, a way capable of holding her, suicide, and God all together in some kind of harmony. I believed it could be done. Sister Mary Ellen had said, "When your daughter died, you can be sure God was there."

Yes, but how? No one could tell me how God was present at Mary's death, and I couldn't simply place the Creator in the middle of Mary's suicide and label the situation "her time to go home." Mental illness brought her down. Everyone knew that, but why was it never enough to know? And why was I always trying to forgive a daughter whose illness seemed to make forgiveness unnecessary? She was beautiful; her death was ugly. There had to be a way of cutting through the senselessness of that reality and retrieving my daughter. I had no intention of saying "I don't understand" for the rest of my life. I yearned to understand. The more I understood, the closer I would be to getting Mary back. I felt that if my pearl dream was any indication, Mary would lead not only to God but also to new life.

My father's decline and death did not, by way of contrast, compel me to launch a search for him. One autumn morning in 1996, I stayed with him while my mother ran errands. He had become increasingly confused and began wandering off to neighboring houses looking for his long-dead mother; and I worried he might try again. Despite his limp, my father could shove anyone, including me, out of his way. But as it happened, he wanted only to look at his garden that Saturday, so we descended back-porch steps into November warmth. Suddenly aware of the urine on his trousers, he said he wanted to stand in the sun and let the wet spot dry. The man who warned me never to look at the sun aimed his eyes directly at it.

"Look at that guy!" he said. "That thing is so big, the government must have put it up there."

"Yeah, Daddy, that's the sun. You shouldn't be looking at it."

"Well, it's heating up my eyes," he said with a laugh, and then with a slight lift of his cane, he added, "Let's go out there."

As we walked past peach trees to the garden, he didn't seem to notice my tears and began a friendly, nonsensical commentary on the plot, now brown brush, that had once yielded corn, tomatoes, butter beans, cantaloupes, and watermelons. On August afternoons, I'd seen him push many a produce-laden wheelbarrow out of that green space.

"Right over there is the corn," he said. "There used to be tomatoes here. But they forgot where they should be."

I peeked under withered tomato vines and was surprised by the mound of tiny white flowers growing beneath.

The sun was playing in and out of the clouds and making the air alternately warm and chilly. After a minute, my father said he wanted to go back to the house. As we were walking back, he stopped, smiled broadly, and scanned the sky. *He's halfway to God.* His garden inspections were coming to an end, had ended years before; but he knew none of that. As a real boy of summer he was taking simple pleasure in the sunlight, and that was consolation enough for me.

When he died four months later, my sister, Joy, remarked, "Daddy's death is sorrowful, but it's not tragic like Mary's."

Sorrow for my father included normal shock, but the shock was mixed with something like happiness. Picking up dry cleaning a day after his passing, I caught myself saying to the proprietor, "My father died yesterday. I have a feeling he's on the glory train."

I liked "glory train" so much I tried it out on several people during the funeral home viewing. I could see my father riding a train of glory. He had the capacity for it.

After the funeral, two dozen of us went back to my mother's house and stood around telling stories about my father, many that made us laugh. My brother, George, told how Daddy had picked dandelions one spring day in the late 1950s at Chimborazo Park in Richmond, Virginia. "It was quite a production, making wine out of those weeds. But the good news is, Mom found one last gallon of it in the basement. What's better than toasting Pops with his own wine?" We poured, lifted glasses in gratitude to God, and drank the tawny brew.

Ray Bradbury writes that the words "dandelion wine" are "summer on the tongue," an evocation of everything good and wonderful about his boyhood.[36] For me that day, dandelion wine embodied the wealth of my father's life. Its sharp sweetness contained all the goodness he received and all the goodness he gave back during his eighty-one years.

Sorrow for my father itself held a kind of sweetness that offered no hint of why seventeen-year-old Mary suffered to the point of death. As I had begun to see, the only way of engaging that question was, in some sense, to live it daily. That meant tiptoeing up to Mary's death—sitting with it, wrestling with it, standing up to it—while also living my life.

Our first Fourth of July without Mary showed how I might go about it. In the morning, Mr. Marshall, our handyman, and his son took apart her bed and hauled mattress, box springs, and frame out to their truck. In ten minutes, they had removed the bed Mary used all her life. I stood by, shoulders tensed, and watched them do it. The bed signified anguish for Mary and for us, it would not be used again; it had to be gotten rid of. Discarding it was a way of standing up to her death—a necessity—and brought forth the usual tears.

But there was life to tend to. So after the truck pulled away, I started baking beans while John Paul whipped up some brownie mix. My mother was coming over for a backyard picnic along with my brother, George, his wife, Rita, and their six-year old Michael. We planned to combine comfort foods, shoot off fireworks, and celebrate an evening that was blue silk—cloudless and brilliant.

It turned out to be a gentle Fourth of July. Watching Michael slice the air with sparklers made me long for distant childhood evenings when I'd run around barefoot and free. Not wanting our celebration to end too quickly, John and Lauren went to a roadside stand and bought more pinwheels and fountains. After the last fountain fizzled, some got tired and wanted to go home, but I doubt anyone would have called the evening tiresome. It was a small triumph of enthusiasm, and it helped me feel safe.

That evening revealed another necessity in the healing search for Mary: silence. No one spoke of Mary on July Fourth, and far from being awkward, it was fitting. I didn't perceive the silence to be repressed anger. I knew family members had been angry—my sister, Joy, for one. But whatever anger there was seemed directed at the crisis of suicide rather than at Mary, John, or me. As far as I could tell, we three had been given the benefit of every doubt and what felt, to me, like deference.

I considered our silence that Fourth of July to be good silence. It wasn't about niceness or strength; it was about sharing loss at a level beyond the reach of words. Borrowing from poet Derek Walcott, I would have described our silence as "sea-deep, earth-deep, love-deep . . . the silence of the deepest buried love."[37] It had a kind of dignity.

My search for Mary required continuing love-deep silence. It was not simply that discussion of my daughter had begun to falter; it had faltered from the first moment. It was not simply that most people had grown uneasy at the mention of her name; they had been uneasy practically from the start. I had recognized frank annoyance in the comment of a friend months before: "When it comes to your daughter, there's nothing more to say." Well, there was plenty more to say, but the time for saying it ended almost before it began. The hard fact of my daughter's suicide and the meaning of her life, the meaning of life itself, forced me to go quiet and take the pain inside where I believed it would be transformed.

It was a positive inward movement, based upon wisdom I'd gleaned from the first Carmelite hermits on Mount Carmel: "In silence and hope shall your strength be."[38] Their rule of silence had endured through nine centuries and gave me hope that if I cast anchor into my own depths, I would find God waiting there to reorient my life in a decent, peaceful way.

A passage from William Maxwell's *Time Will Darken It* portrays an "age of quiet" passing over a home one afternoon, over the "richness contained in cupboards, the serenity of objects in empty rooms." Maxwell describes how the sunlight "relinquished its hold on the corner of an oriental rug . . . in order to warm the leg of a chair. . . . [A] single white wheel-shaped phlox blossom hung for a long time and then dropped to the table without making a sound."[39] In my house, I observed the sunlight and watched the blossom drop. At my window, I noticed tiny shadows on my hand when leaves fell through autumn sunshine. There was fullness in the light and shadow, a kind of healing holiness I couldn't help noticing.

In Mary's bedroom, I sat on the floor and went through her things, one by one: sorting, boxing, and discarding. *Everything must go. She will not be back to claim a single item, no.* For a few minutes at a time, it was not too bad a job. I took comfort in the perfumed turquoise sweater, the worn-down lipstick, the cotton balls and doodads. I glanced through dozens of birthday cards she'd received and placed in a red and gold box. They all wished her many more birthdays and told of love, admiration, and happiness at having her for a cousin, a niece, a granddaughter.

There was also a handwritten letter John had given her in 1991 on the night of her confirmation. "You are one of the more joy-filled experiences of my life," he wrote. "Your sweetness and spirit of obedience are so very much appreciated. Your fine abilities in school, attractive personality, and good sense of humor hide a more quiet side which looks into things and wonders about them."

MARY AT THE BARTON GARNET MINE, 1990.

I picked up her high school yearbook and turned to the autographed pages, trying to figure out how she had gotten along with classmates: "Love you," one inscription said. "Have a blast this summer. You made biology bearable." All were good-humored and out of kilter. After a while, the yearbook scribbles were absurd, the vacant room was absurd, and Mary's death was absurd all over again.

On at least a couple of occasions, I would have quit the packing job and gone downstairs except for one thing: Mary's presence to me in that bedroom was real; it glowed with reality. There was nothing supernatural about her presence; it was more my awareness that she still cared about me. At first, her death had seemed cavalier and reckless, an abandonment of everything meaningful in our lives together, an abandonment of me. Yet in the silence of her room, I started believing, and I still believe that Mary was urging me onward to a truer self.

Because the shock of grief was wearing into deep loneliness, I began to think a truer self might come about through better human connections. Though touchy as sunburn and unready for merriment, I told myself that greater investment in relationship might take away my loneliness, balance the silence, and give me back myself. I had the companionship of John and other family members, it's true, but they were occupied with their own grief.

Besides, I needed to get away from the "suicide survivor" label occasionally and reestablish myself as a regular person. So I arranged lunches with accomplished, admirable women who, despite their own struggles, knew how to laugh. My personal guidelines for these new relationships ruled out grief talk. I felt if I refrained from unloading grief, the other person might catch the spirit and we could then have fun. That often happened. As it turned out, an hour of lunchtime breeziness usually gave way to an evening of inner dreariness, but I passed that off to the quirkiness of grief and kept going.

My intoxication with good cheer ended after several months when a friend said she couldn't get together with me for a long time and, no, she wouldn't discuss it, a dismissal I sensed coming even as I denied its possibility. That relationship failure stung with humiliation and intensified my sadness for Mary. But at least it got me to admit I'd been trying to coax people into the Mary-void, which wasn't theirs to fill and which could not, in any case, be filled. It also prompted greater respect for the position grief had put me in: roughed up and vulnerable.

The good news was that I finally did grasp my situation with a clear head. Loneliness was the way it was going to be for a while. It gnawed like hunger, but I found I could live with it. I could sit with it, stand up to it, and not run from it. I could even believe God was at the center of it, helping in ways I could not understand.

Not understanding and not knowing gradually became a kind of strength. Psalm 139 captures something of the divine enigma drawing my attention: "If I say, 'Surely the darkness shall hide me, and night shall be my light' / For you darkness itself is not dark, and night shines as the day."[10] The mysterious "beyondness" of God in Scripture and in life, hardly to be disputed, began to light my way obscurely.

At Washington Theological Union, every course I took over the years seemed to offer a handle of one or two memorable phrases that guided me long after the class ended. In my class on the writings of John of the Cross, one of the handles that emerged concerned unknowing. "To reach union with the wisdom of God," John wrote, "a person must advance by un-knowing rather than by knowing."[11] Having spent a semester wading through the Mystical Doctor's teachings, I latched onto "We advance by unknowing" as an unexpected boon. It was portable. I could carry the phrase; perhaps it would carry me.

Maybe my inability to know what happened to Mary, and how and where God was in relationship to her and me—maybe that inability was not a lack but a benefit if it was getting me to walk by faith. Perhaps it was unknowing that would lead to God and to Mary. But adjusting to the idea was not easy. Of all my grieving tasks, owning up to blindness and giving way to God's deep mysteriousness were among the most arduous. I expressed that view in one of my exam papers before adding, "I have fallen forcefully into Mystery that I can dimly 'know' but cannot control or understand."

To amplify the point, I then inserted words of theologian Michael Buckley, which I thought true, beautiful, and impossible of improvement: "Mystery is not what I do not know. I do know it. I know it as Mystery, as the final context of my life. . . . Mystery is not that which I cannot know. Mystery is that which I cannot exhaust, which I cannot go beyond, which I cannot transcend."[12] It was Mystery that I said (and believed) gave loving context to Mary's life. I expected that simply embracing the idea of Mystery would bring an end to the search for my daughter. Her suicide could finally be stirred into the cauldron of Mystery and made to disappear.

One thing I was not expecting at that time was an invitation to parish ministry. I received a letter from Father Joe asking if I would train to become a eucharistic minister, and I said I would. All Saints needed some fifty parishioners to help distribute holy communion at nine weekend Masses, so I recognized the obligation of serving as well as the sacredness of it. I had seen gladness in the faces of eucharistic ministers on many occasions, and I was hoping for that gladness.

During a training session a man said, "Standing in front of the church and giving out the Eucharist is not about us. It's about Jesus." His words sounded holy enough, and no one disagreed with them. But I thought he was wrong. *The Eucharist is not about Jesus, it is Jesus. We're not robots but living participants.*

One Sunday a month, I took the Blessed Sacrament to nursing-home residents who were no longer able to attend Mass. On those Sundays I arrived at the church between Masses, placed the required number of eucharistic wafers in a small container called a pyx, which I carried in a leather case around my neck, and drove a mile in silence to Annaburg Manor. With my list of residents who were Catholic and their room numbers, I began on the ground floor where the more able residents lived and worked my way up to the second and third floors.

The first person I visited was Dorothy. No matter what the hour, Dorothy was nicely made up, brightly dressed, and smiling. Her half of the room contained an abundance of window plants and stuffed animals. "How are *you?*" she asked, and because she was a patient of John's, "How's the doctor?" Sometimes she spoke of her daughter; sometimes she complained about her wheelchair. Opening my *Pastoral Care of the Sick* book of rites, I greeted her once again: "The peace of the Lord be with you always."

"And also with you," she responded.

After a reading from the Gospel of John, we prayed the Our Father together. I then offered communion to Dorothy who accepted it, saying, "Amen."

Over the following thirty minutes, half a dozen residents on the first floor also received communion. The disposition with which they received it remained, of course, interior and hidden. One woman named Elizabeth always cried during the Our Father but would gather herself after a moment and thank me.

Patients on the second floor were undergoing physical rehabilitation of some sort. The entire floor was a place of frailty: pale people in mechanized beds connected to oxygen tanks with plastic tubes running under their blankets. Many were too weak to pray aloud, so I prayed for them, even the responses. Many had difficulty swallowing, so the smallest piece of communion wafer was all I'd offer.

One young woman couldn't swallow at all. Michelle was in her twenties and had brain damage from a car accident. She lay comatose on a respirator, her face bloated and waxen. Though I tried to steady myself, seeing Michelle every month shocked me. *If Mary had lived, she would be lying here on a respirator like this poor girl. She would be lying here day after day between life and death. And it would be her own doing.*

After tracing a cross on Michelle's arm, I leaned in to pray the Our Father, the leather eucharistic case suspended on its cord between us. She could not receive the Eucharist, but I wanted it to be near her for a moment. There had been a time in my life when I wanted to receive the Eucharist and could not receive it. That was the seven-year interval after I met John and before I entered the Catholic Church.

When John and I went to Mass on Sundays during those years, I remained in the pew as he stood in the communion line—a separation that seemed harsh and out of keeping with love. Now I believe that eucharistic grace was flowing through me during those Masses and luring me into community even if I couldn't perceive it at the time. I was being brought into light and truth, and now I hoped that light and truth were being brought into Michelle.

It was a hope I carried up to residents of the third floor, the locked ward where Alzheimer's patients wandered through days and nights looking for a way out of the place. I was familiar with the third floor. I was familiar with the broccoli-and-Lysol smell, the shout-outs from residents in the halls, the blare of television news. My father had lived on that floor for two months before he died. He was usually ambling down the shiny corridor when I visited. Once I fell in step and ambled along with him, my arm around him and his around me. While looking for him in someone's room one day, I watched a woman with long gray hair shuffle by. She was saying over and over, "I just want to kill somebody." It was not an unusual level of agitation.

When I approached Catholics on the third floor to ask if they would like to receive the Eucharist, most could not answer. They usually just stared, sometimes pleasantly. I would take the pyx from the leather case and hold it up, saying, "Would you like to receive the Eucharist?" If that offer met with silence, I'd remove a communion wafer and show it to them. Often the sight of the simple white wafer broke through dementia to depths of grace, and many did say yes. They closed their eyes and entered into Christ's death and resurrection.

I won't claim it was an orderly arrangement. Commotion surrounded us in the corridor. Occasionally, communicants agreed to have a piece of wafer placed on their tongues and then, forgetting how to swallow, spit it out—a real misjudgment on my part. At those moments, I told myself we were all doing our best and wondered, probably defensively, what more could be expected.

In my search for human connection during those years, a nursing home was the last place I would have looked. I was also not looking for answers to questions about Mary, suicide, and God among the elderly of those ancient hallways. Someone had to take communion to the people on fourth Sundays of the month, and I was asked to do so. My duty was to show up with the sacred bread and a little human warmth, after which I could go back to my nice family Sabbath.

But as those fourth Sundays accumulated, I felt a shift taking place. Instead of merely receiving what was bestowed upon them, residents were delivering compassion to me in tiny doses. A few asked about John and the children each month. Some tried to make me feel all right about leaving their rooms when I could tell they wanted me to stay. "Don't you worry, honey," Dorothy said one morning. "I know you've got a lot of people on that list." They seemed to appreciate my intentions and excuse my limitations. Over time, it was their gentleness that softened my sharp focus on the ways I'd failed Mary.

On any given Sunday, one or two Catholic residents lay near death, delicate and helpless, blankets drawn up to their chins. Standing beside Ruth one April Sunday, I thought she would be gone by the time I came back in May. Eighty-six and slight, pallid, and white-robed, Ruth didn't see me by her bed that day but, like my father during our garden walk, she surely must have been seeing something of God. Holiness, a depth of presence both powerful and unfathomable, was written in her small face. Her dying would have seemed opposite to my daughter's except for one thing: it evoked something of the awe and fear I felt at seeing Mary on her deathbed.

It brought to mind a theological term I once heard in Professor Manning's class: *mysterium tremendum et fascinans* (mystery that repels and fascinates). The religious philosopher Rudolph Otto used the phrase to describe the ambivalence (the reverence, impotence, fascination) we feel in the presence of the Holy.[43] I experienced holiness in Ruth's dying and, though far more difficult, also imagined holiness in Mary's dying. That was the gift.

Around that time, John Paul agreed to move his bed and all his possessions into Mary's vacant room. He said he wasn't bothered by the idea of taking over her room. But I think he was trying to do a nice thing by allowing his old bedroom to be turned into something new: a computer room for the rest of us. Finally, we could rid the upstairs of its empty bedroom feel and enter into the computer era like everyone else. For our twenty-fifth wedding anniversary in 1997, my mother gave us our first big, beige desktop computer, which my brother, George, spent an afternoon helping me set up.

Before long, a new computer in a new space began generating a new hope: *I'm ready to write about Mary*. My mother had told me throughout the early grieving, "Someday, you'll write about all this." By that she meant Mary's death, as though there was good to be brought out of it.

"No, I'm not writing a book about Mary," I replied. The idea of turning her death into a writing project depressed me, though I thought it might eventually stop depressing me. Somewhere in my head, the idea of two years began to take hold. Two years would provide healing. Two years would provide enough distance to go beyond handwritten journals and word process my way to clarity. Now those two years were drawing to a close, and I decided to begin. I had the computer, I had the space, I had the time, and I thought I had the gumption.

That year, the month of May was quiet around our house because John Paul was working at a grocery store and Lauren was still in school. But the silence didn't keep me from closing the door and turning off the phone when I went into the computer room. I was going there to be with Mary. I had to think about our last summer together, no matter what emerged, and I had to write about it. I was seeking relationship with my daughter, all sweet calm and reason, as though our troubles might be over.

I started by asking Mary why she'd substituted journal writing for human contact and spent the last few minutes of her life writing: "You went out not fighting, but writing." I asked if writing had been her way of making sense of a life that increasingly made no sense. I recounted the story Father Joe told at her funeral about Puccini's death and the unfinished opera that one of Puccini's students completed. I then asked if she'd want me to round out her unfinished story. Within seconds of asking the question, I knew the answer. "Perhaps you're waiting for me to write you back into life," I noted. Maybe there was to be a relationship, at least in my memories, and maybe it was time for me to bring it about.

That notion turned out to be pretty naïve. In one sense, I already knew life in the memory realm would keep me living in the past. I had read what John of the Cross has to say about memory. While studying *The Ascent of Mount Carmel* three months before, I had underlined John's advice regarding memory and written "Mary Kathryn" beside it. "Do not store objects of hearing, sight, smell, taste, or touch in the memory," John of the Cross wrote, "but leave them immediately and forget them, and endeavor, if necessary, to be as successful in forgetting them as others are in remembering them."[44]

So even then I had an inkling that memories of Mary must give way to hope in God, the past for the future, as John of the Cross teaches. I suspected that memories, beautiful though they might be, were not the foundation upon which I could build a relationship with my daughter. They were not of the essence to which I was called: freedom here and now in God's presence.

Just the same, I wanted to dwell upon memories of Mary, no matter what John of the Cross advised. I wanted to get down on paper some of the moments she and I shared her last summer. I wanted to write about the peace, orderliness, and happiness of those months, such as the way she threw her head back and laughed hard at some crazy stunt she saw a waiter perform while she was working at the North China Inn. I wanted to record the day in July she had all of her wisdom teeth surgically removed. I wanted to praise her for making all the necessary appointments and to remind myself I would not have done the same at the age of seventeen.

My recollections of that summer emphasized relationship, so I described putting my arm around her at the oral surgeon's office when I saw how scared she was and how, once she was situated in a back room, I went to fill her Darvon prescription, buy chocolate ice cream, and rent a movie. I remembered that, upon returning to the doctor's office, I parked in the shade so Mary wouldn't have to ride home in a hot car. *How glad I am we closed the blinds in my bedroom, got on the bed, and watched the movie together that day.* Yes, I was glad for that, but remembering it was akin to watching a diamond ring wash down a sink drain.

Even so, I kept trying to remember. I wrote about our trip to Mary Washington College in Fredericksburg, Virginia, on a muggy August day. I recalled the sky that morning as low and gray, threatening rain, and Mary watching out the window during the drive. Because we were visiting the college from which

I graduated, I recalled that my energy level had risen considerably. I remembered finding someone in the administration building to answer admissions questions and seeing how pleased Mary was at the idea of majoring in French and living in the French house.

I allowed that the nicest part of the day for me was walking to the wooded amphitheater and pointing to a beech tree bearing my carved initials. A Peruvian marine from Quantico, Virginia, had put them there in 1969. I remembered wanting Mary to see them and to know I hadn't always been a white-bread mom. I had hoped we might bond around that small disclosure; and while glancing at the tree, Mary said, "Wow, that's something." But she didn't josh with me as I hoped she would.

My memory exercises ended after three weeks. Instead of bringing about relationship, they brought about fear. I feared what I would find if I continued digging into memory. *What I might learn about you, Mary, are things I don't want to know and never did want to know. I might find the real dimensions of your inability to be who we thought you were. I might come to see your giftedness that was wrecked by illness, a giftedness the loss of which makes us all poor and needy. There might be the sense of tragedy written large and incomprehensibly. How on earth? How could I let someone like you slip right through my fingers?*

Endnotes

35 Emily Dickinson, *The Complete Poems*, 143.

36 Ray Bradbury, *Dandelion Wine* (New York: Bantam Books, 1975), 13.

37 Derek Walcott, "Oddjob, a Bull Terrier," *Derek Walcott Collected Poems 1948-1984* (New York: Farrar, Straus & Giroux, 1986), 335.

38 St. Albert of Jerusalem, *The Carmelite Rule of Saint Albert* (Washington, DC: Washington Province of the Immaculate Heart of Mary, 2012), 5.

39 William Maxwell, *Time Will Darken It* (New York: Vintage Books, 1997), 94.

40 Psalm 139, *The New American Bible* (Wichita, Kansas: Catholic Book Publishing Co., 1983), 646.

41 St. John of the Cross, *The Collected Works of Saint John of the* Cross, trans. Kieran Kavanaugh, O.C.D., and Otilio Rodriguez, O.C.D. (Washington, DC: ICS Publications, 1991), 126.

42 Michael J. Buckley, "Within the Holy Mystery," *A World of Grace*, ed. Leo J. O'Donovan (Washington, DC: Georgetown University Press, 1995), 40.

43 Rudolf Otto, *The Idea of the Holy* trans. John W. Harvey (London: Oxford University Press, 1958), 31.

44 St. John of the Cross, *Collected Works*, 272.

10

BEFRIENDING

But some day, hidden by His will,
if this meek child is waiting still,
God will take out His mercy-key
and open up felicity
JESSICA POWERS[45]

JUST AFTER THE NEW YEAR'S Eve ball descended into Times Square at the stroke of 2000, my mother whispered to me, "I hope this is a better year for you."

Some twenty family members and friends had put on party clothes and gathered at my sister's home for dinner that December evening. Candles flickered and television satellites beamed global revels into our celebration. Despite widespread concern about computer systems seizing up at midnight and plunging the world into chaos, power grids seemed to be holding and airplanes were reported to be flying normally: reason enough for cheer and champagne.

More than four years had passed since Mary's death, and while sorrow lingered just beneath the surface of family get-togethers and occasionally made an appearance, it no longer put a drag on good spirits. Mostly there were signs of mutual respect at the New Year's Eve party—small courtesies, really, for what we'd all gone through together. After years of distress, my entire family apparently still believed in its own goodness.

When my mother whispered, "I hope this is a better year for you," I felt she was probably hoping I'd complete a final academic project that likely seemed odd or even tormenting to her: a master's thesis with "suicide" in the title, "The Relationship Between Suicide and Community in the Roman Catholic Tradition." At the beginning of my academic program in 1994, I'd been informed that in order to graduate I would have to write a long research paper under the direction of a faculty member. After Mary died, there was no question in my mind that the focus of the paper would be suicide. Even after four years, I was still thinking about my daughter every hour. In truth, she was like a small engine in my brain that I couldn't turn off.

My other interest was, of course, the various communities that had been with us in the middle of our adversity. In those dreadful waiting moments at the emergency room on the afternoon of Mary's death, I was telling myself: *John and I were with people all day, but Mary was alone in her room. At the very moment we were surrounded by community she was cutting herself off. What can that possibly mean?*

During the week of wake and funeral I began to say, "If John and I had been at a party on Sunday instead of a monastery, Mary's death would be different. Not that there's anything wrong with parties, but it matters that we were in community. Our Carmelite community was with Mary in prayer. I can't understand it, but I don't believe she was ever really alone."

For mental stability, I had to believe it. But I also held to the words of commendation that Father Dave prayed for us at the hour of Mary's death. They were full of community. They spoke of her going forth from this world in the name of the Father, Son, and Holy Spirit and living in peace this day, the day of her death, with the Blessed Virgin, Joseph, and all the angels and saints. Those words cut with terrible beauty, strange and unforgettable.

Along with that realization came the feeling that suicide and community were somehow linked together inside my 5-foot-4-inch frame. Without conscious reference to Christ's cross I would hold out one arm and say to myself: "Here's community"; and then the other: "Here's suicide. They're part of me, and I can't make them not be part of me."

When the date arrived in 1999 for committing to a thesis topic, I had no real qualms about investigating how the church has dealt with suicide throughout its history. I knew I'd largely be unearthing ecclesial condemnations of the act, but I also knew that the 1994 *Catechism of the Catholic Church* treated suicide sensitively. Not only did it acknowledge that psychological disturbance, anguish, and grave fear can diminish personal responsibility for suicide, but it also urged hope for the salvation of suicide victims.[46] The *Catechism* gave me shelter. No matter how upsetting historical church language about suicide might prove to be, and I already had an idea of it, at least the *Catechism* provided enlightened, present-day reassurance.

In taking on suicide as a thesis topic, though, what heartened me most was my experience of community, those mourners who had overcome their natural abhorrence of suicide and waited in line at the funeral home to talk with John and me. Their presence was and had always been a thing apart, in power and delicacy beyond any social connection I had ever experienced, a high point in my life.

So I thought I could prove to myself (if no one else) that God was present to my daughter in those mourners. I wanted to prove to myself that All Saints parishioners were a sign of salvation for her. I wanted everyone's kindness to represent—moreover, *be*—God's kindness in delivering my daughter from despair and death. But I didn't dare reveal those desires, at least not in the beginning. They were private and maternal, and the research and writing required facts and objectivity.

I pitched my ideas about suicide and community to Professor Martha Manning who agreed to direct the thesis. Throughout the previous several semesters, she'd sat and listened to my conjectures about daughter, suicide, and God. "I don't think God calls people home through suicide," she'd once told me. Her comment squeezed the air out of me because, incredibly, I'd not heard it before. But it also cleared away some of my bewilderment and helped me see that I could learn to think coherently about God and suicide if I worked at it.

"If you do decide to go with this suicide and community idea," she said, "you'll have to look at the entire church tradition on suicide, beginning with Scripture. You'll also have to define 'Roman Catholic community' and how our understanding of it has evolved. Those are a couple of the basics. Let's see it in writing."

I submitted the proposal exactly along those lines, got it approved, and moved my books into the computer room, now a sanctuary containing family pictures, my daughter Mary's patent leather tap shoes, a copper Celtic cross, and a fist-sized gray rock. John's brother Robert had given us the cross for Christmas years earlier, and my eyes rested on it every time I looked up from the computer screen. The rock was one Lauren found at the Barton Garnet Mine when we were vacationing one summer in the Adirondacks. It was dull gray except for a chipped place revealing maroon crystals through and through, a mystery the cool weight of which I wanted near my hand.

One thing was clear right from the beginning of my writing venture: I was done talking. When Sister Mary Ellen told me, "You need your friends," I didn't disagree; but I wasn't going to waste time talking when I had such a vital project looming. In fact, I didn't need friends. I needed to take on the loneliness that goes with suicide, to accept and befriend it, because I couldn't see it ever completely receding. I needed John and the kids giving me encouragement. I especially needed prayers from the living and the dead, that community of love just beyond me but also silently near.

As I began to wade knee-deep into the study of suicide and community, I found myself standing tall in hope. That was a new sensation, because most of my suicide study over the years had been like watching television crime shows in which the dead are displayed as curiosities. The books about suicide I'd been reading neither mentioned God nor spoke of the death of real human beings. Instead, the authors discussed suicide as a medical failure or served up philosophy regarding the disposal of one's life or presented statistics about time, place, and method of self-destruction. Those books were dry, whereas my daughter's death had been bloody and full of tears.

But when I looked into the New Testament, I found a heartening sequence of events, beginning in the Acts of the Apostles with Paul's jailer. He drew his sword to kill himself after waking to see the prison doors open and Paul and Silas apparently free. But Paul evangelized him instead of condemning him. The jailer's family was then baptized, after which the jailer ". . . led them up into his house, spread a table before them, and joyfully celebrated with his whole family his newfound faith in God" (16:33-34). The family meal shared in "jubilant gladness" was, according to *The New Jerome Biblical Commentary*, a sign of salvation received.[47] For me, such an interpretation was almost too good to be true.

When I came across Augustine's fourth-century denunciation of suicide, the most influential in history, I couldn't help noting its ecclesial and cultural context. Weighing into Augustine's denunciation, for example, were the schismatic Donatists of North Africa. Some roamed the countryside claiming to be the authentically pure and holy church, even killing themselves in heroic protest to the opposition they encountered in the Roman Catholic Church. As bishop of Hippo, Augustine condemned their self-destruction as a sinful violation of the Christian virtue of endurance under trial.

The sack of Rome in AD 410 occasioned a fuller treatment of suicide by Augustine. When pagans blamed the city's ruin on Christians for supposedly bringing about a decline in the worship of traditional gods, Augustine wrote *Concerning the City of God against the Pagans* as encouragement for those Christians. He made clear that life in Christ requires virtuous living, not dying by one's own hand, and that the killing of oneself is the killing of a human being and thus prohibited by the fifth commandment.[48]

I could hardly disagree with Augustine's accent on virtuous living and the ultimate value of human life, although I did wonder what it had to do with my daughter's suicide. She practiced virtue and cherished life; and as her mother, I deeply knew it. I would have argued with anyone who tried to say otherwise.

But in the end, I did find some of Augustine's teachings about the church helpful to my understanding of suicide and community. He taught that church community is populated by good and bad Christians, grain and chaff, and is a locus of healing and holiness. "Anyone who grows cold in love is sick in the body of Christ," he preached. "But God . . . has the power to heal the sick members provided they haven't amputated themselves by extreme wickedness. . . . [W]hatever remains in the body need not despair of being restored to health. . . ."[49]

It's true that I felt my daughter had taken an ax and cut herself off from everyone, but I never considered hers to be an act of "extreme wickedness." I believed from the first that she had remained in the Body of Christ or, more precisely, that the Body of Christ had remained in her, not that I could have proven it in a thesis.

My research also included the works of Thomas Aquinas in the thirteenth century, in which I found that his first and third reasons for prohibiting suicide were not unfamiliar ones. They addressed the human responsibility of loving and cherishing oneself, along with the responsibility of recognizing God as giver of life with power over life and death. It was Aquinas's second argument against suicide, however, that prompted my gratitude, partly because it hadn't appeared earlier in church tradition and partly because I'd experienced its legitimacy. Suicide, Aquinas wrote, "does injury to the community to which each [person] belongs as part of the whole."[50]

But was Aquinas willing to grant that community could heal such an injury? From my reading, the answer was not entirely clear. Yves Congar claims that Aquinas's "first and deepest" idea of the church was that of Mystical Body, new life in Christ for all through the Holy Spirit.[51] But that inward mode of church required a holy, outward expression through the hierarchy. Because at that time bishops and religious alone were charged with the responsibility of pursuing spiritual perfection on behalf of the entire church, the people of God were no longer considered in themselves a center of holiness capable of delivering salvation.

I began to see that the following seven centuries of church life were marked by an increasingly decisive denunciation of suicide that was centered on the concept of law and penalty. The Council of Trent during the sixteenth century, for example, held that the law forbids suicide and that no one possesses such power over his life as to end it. Throughout my Protestant childhood, I was influenced by that teaching. To my young mind, the law was God's law, and the penalty for breaking the law was hell. Up through the early decades of the twentieth century, in fact, the church taught that Christians who broke God's law by choosing death removed themselves in every way from the spiritual jurisdiction of the church. Suicide severed Christian communion, and those who committed suicide were considered as lost.[52]

But divine love was always running like garnet crystals just beneath that judgment, and no church pronouncements could conceal it forever. In one of her last conversations before dying in 1897, St. Thérèse of Lisieux, for example, made this luminous remark to Mother Agnes, her prioress: "One could believe that it is because I haven't sinned that I have such great confidence in God. Really tell them, Mother, that if I had committed all possible crimes, I would always have the same confidence; I feel that this whole multitude of offenses would be like a drop of water thrown into a fiery furnace."[53]

"All possible crimes" and "great confidence in God" got my attention when I came across those phrases during the summer of 1997. I'd begun the summer trying to write about my daughter Mary only to find myself stalled by fear. But then I turned to Thérèse of Lisieux, the French Discalced Carmelite saint who had died a century before at the age of 24.

Word out of Rome in 1997 was that St. Thérèse was going to be named a Doctor of the Church in recognition of her outstanding doctrine and distinguished holiness. In consideration of that, I was asked to write a Carmelite study guide for her memoir, *The Story of a Soul*, in which she set forth her "little way" of confidence in God as Merciful Love.[54]

Ill with tuberculosis and physically incapable of climbing a "rough stairway of perfection" to heroic sanctity, Thérèse wrote of trying to return God's unconditional love in all the little ways that made up her day. While acknowledging her littleness and imperfection, Thérèse focused on the benevolent love she believed God had always lavished and would always lavish upon her, no matter what. In fact, she maintained that it was precisely her flaws and helplessness that along with trust in God made the greatest claim on divine compassion.

In her suicide note, my daughter Mary had written, "I was weak, and I hated myself."

But Thérèse was telling me in her memoir: "I am weak, and God loves me." Hers was a stirring shift of emphasis from sin and human imperfection to the "fiery furnace" of God's abundant love. I kept in mind Thérèse's boldness when I was writing the suicide thesis two years later. It ended up fortifying me against the church's condemnations as I read large books and tried, underneath it all, to make sense of my daughter's dreadful end.

MARY, LAUREN, AND MARJ AT MARY'S EIGHTH-GRADE GRADUATION, 1992.

In April 2000, I submitted the thesis draft to Martha Manning and Robert McCaslin, a moral theology professor. When those five dozen pages finally gained approval, they filled me with something like reverence. I didn't let them out of my sight for days. When I delivered them to the UPS store for copying and binding, though, the clerk behind the counter let me know what he thought of the title: "Guilt, guilt!"

"What? You mean 'suicide and Roman Catholic'? Nah, the church is more compassionate now"—hardly a groundbreaking comment. Father Dave had said the same thing five years earlier on the night of Mary's death. It wasn't much for me to offer, considering all I'd learned during the year of writing a thesis. But I was standing in a store with a stranger that day. The real suicide conversation would take place a few days later as I sat for an hour in a classroom with Professors Martha and Robert.

That conversation was known as defending the thesis, and it required me to make a prepared statement and then answer questions. I figured Martha and Robert would be looking for clarification here and there but mostly for a reflection about the project's meaning, which had shifted in my mind by the time I'd completed the research. What had begun to seem more compelling than suicide and community was the question of God and innocent suffering, though I was just beginning to recognize it as a question and far from able to articulate it.

I arrived early at the Union on the day of my thesis defense and sat in a passageway, staring at the blue shoe on my left foot. Six years of study, classes, and Beltway-driving would be over in sixty minutes, and I wanted to feel happy about it. What I felt instead was heat rising in my face and a kind of angry resolve. My daughter deserved to be included in the upcoming discussion;

and after nine months of buttoned-down, academic writing, I was going to include her.

Eventually, I heard laughter in the stairwell, which became louder as Martha and Robert drew nearer. *Where do they get off laughing at a time like this?* But, of course, why shouldn't they laugh? They were climbing stairs to fulfill an hour's responsibility after which they could put the topic of suicide behind them. I wouldn't be putting suicide behind me anytime soon. My daughter was involved in it, and so was God.

Martha, Robert, and I sat down behind tables facing each other in a small classroom. I began by saying my husband had encouraged me to write about suicide one morning at breakfast. "And I also wanted to write about my experience of community. By that, I mean not only the liturgical and pastoral care my family received but also the presence of parishioners, Carmelites, as well as students and faculty here at the Union. There was a willingness to share in the suffering that was wonderfully compassionate and gracious." Martha and Robert smiled in encouragement.

"In my research, I found two statements particularly powerful. The first comes from ecclesiologist J.-M. R. Tillard. In 1992, he wrote: 'The gestures by which Jesus accomplishes and signifies the breakthrough of the Kingdom are precisely gestures of the tenderness and compassion of God towards the poor.'"

"And then Tillard adds, 'the field of poverty keeps getting larger [to include] men and women who are perhaps well off [materially] . . . but troubled in their minds or human relationships, plunging them into misery.'"[55]

Setting aside my notes I said, "The field of poverty keeps getting larger, and it includes those who die by suicide. Who is more troubled or defeated? Surely they must be counted among the poor through whom the kingdom of God breaks into human consciousness."

My daughter had been an innocent child made poor by illness, and the tenderness my family received after her death was divine. That was what I really wanted to tell Martha and Robert. But it was too personal a remark, and just thinking about it made my throat hurt.

"The second statement to highlight comes from an address Pope John Paul II delivered in 1988. He was visiting Mauthausen, a Nazi concentration camp in Austria, when he said, 'You people who have experienced fearful tortures . . . what is your last word? . . . Tell us, in our great hurry, haven't we forgotten your hell? Aren't we extinguishing traces of great crimes in our memories and consciousness?

. . . Speak, you have the right to do so—you who have suffered and lost your lives. We have the duty to listen to your testimony '"[56]

I had been surprised by the Holy Father's remarks at Mauthausen: his refusal to rationalize, spiritualize, or talk away innocent human suffering. His words struck a tuning fork that still hummed inside my chest. They told me that no matter what anyone might say to the contrary, a mother shouldn't try to forget her daughter's hell.

"So this thesis has attempted to overcome the silence surrounding suicide. It has attempted to give voice to those who suffer and who, by choice, lose their lives. It is really my attempt to listen to what a daughter was trying to say and to what God might be saying through her."

Martha and Robert were silent for a moment. Then they took turns asking whether suicide occurs in Hebrew Scripture and whether there's a link between Catholic community and the guilt to which Catholic suicide survivors seem prone. We went back and forth on those and other issues, which I treated respectfully even though they were off the point. The point was God and my daughter—the God of love and the impoverished, suffering daughter. That was the only question I cared about.

My dissatisfaction with the line of questioning must have shown. Near the end of the hour Robert complained, "Where's the resurrection in this thesis?"

Pointing to my heart, I said, "It's right here." *Haven't you understood?*

The exam ended in laughter a little later with Martha saying, "See you at graduation!"

I thanked her and Robert, bowing slightly. "Suicide is a deeply offensive and repugnant act," I said, while standing to leave. *No one should forget that.*

Yet, I did forget it for a while. On the night of graduation, I put aside thoughts of my daughter and enjoyed the family members who were celebrating with me. My mother had suffered a mild heart attack the week before and was recovering at home. But John, John Paul, Lauren, my brother, George, and Sister Mary Ellen turned out. They all stood on the steps of Nativity Catholic Church with smiles on their faces as we lined up for the procession. It was exhilarating. During the ceremony, sixteen-year-old Lauren told John, to his delight, "I'm going to do this too. I'm going to get a master's degree, and then I'm going to get a doctorate."

When graduates were finally sent into the needy world that May night, I felt a keen obligation to return something to God for the classmates, professors, and studies, which, as my mother put it, had been my salvation all those grieving years.

My first official chance at giving back to God appeared in the form of a phone call from the director of the Carmelite studies program at Washington Theological Union. He asked if I'd consider teaching in that program the following spring. The opportunity thrilled me. Both John and my mother whooped when they heard the news and said that teaching would be a good thing, a wonderful thing. I couldn't foresee what a complicated thing it would be because, even after five years of grief work, I had still more work to do.

An analysis of "The Ugly Duckling" fable in *Women Who Run with the Wolves* eventually helped me understand my situation. The author, Clarissa Estés, claims that mothers who give birth to an "ugly duckling" child always run the danger of becoming outcasts in their communities.[57] I certainly hadn't been made an outcast. But the complete otherness of Mary's behavior—the disgrace and sorrow of it, the terrible damage of it—put a skittishness in me. As the mother of a taboo-breaking daughter, I felt not only ill at ease with people who knew about Mary but also phony toward those who didn't know, as if I were hiding a huge personal secret from them.

It was now obvious that Mary's death had pulled me in several directions. I had been pulled away from her for the sake of my survival at the very time I was being pulled toward her out of love. The tension of those pulls destabilized me from the start. In truth, a whirlpool of defiance for my survival, love for my daughter, and fear for my family dragged me down early and often in the months after Mary died.

There was one psychic pull, however, that I hadn't recognized: my longing for readmission to the community of the whole, the trustworthy, and the accountable. Estés describes it as the desire of an "ugly duckling" mother to be accepted by her "village" and contends that a mother will often "bend to the desires of her village rather than align herself with her child." [58] The invitation to teach at the Union turned out to be the village acceptance I had been unconsciously seeking for five years. It worked a kind of magic on me that eventually devolved, nevertheless, into fear.

Fear of not being accepted by the students had me arriving at the Union two hours early, eating a cold sandwich in the car, and standing at the copier printing assignments for adults who could have done that job themselves. It was fear that kept me holed up at home with those same assignments trying to stay two pages ahead. Unable to relax, I would catch myself striding rather than walking through the house.

"I don't want to look like an idiot in front of the students," I told Sister Mary Ellen.

"Well, you know you're not an idiot," she said.

Even so, I sensed I'd taken a wrong step in life.

Despite my misgivings, the students did seem to be getting something from the class. At the end of the semester, the Carmelite studies director called me to his office and said I could teach the following spring if I wanted to. I said I did. At that moment, what I mostly wanted was to be accepted as someone worthy of teaching.

But in the following several thousand moments, I began to care less about acceptance and more about the daughter I'd turned away from in order to stand at a lectern. It started to bother me that I'd not mentioned Mary in class a single time even when I might have done so. I could have mentioned her while discussing St. Teresa of the Andes dying at the age of nineteen and breaking every heart. I knew the desolation of a young woman's death; but saying how I knew would have been unprofessional, so I didn't say.

Once the semester ended, that decision weighed on me like betrayal. I'd tried to gain acceptance by dispensing with my daughter; that was clear to me. I'd pretended for a while that her suicide was a past event and not the event through which I was seeing every other event and where, most certainly, God was appearing as through a dark glass. So I gathered up every piece of course material lying around the computer room, boxed it up, and got it out of sight. *I have a duty, and I'm going to do it.*

My duty was to go into that computer room every summer day and write down whatever I could remember about the week of Mary's death. I owed my daughter that little bit of dedication. Writing about her death might also bring peace with her and with God, which had so far eluded me. In the six years following her death, I'd celebrated birthdays, baptisms, weddings, and wedding anniversaries. I'd attended wakes and funerals, classes, and spiritual direction. I'd vacationed with my family in the mountains and at the beach. I'd distributed thousands of communion hosts, all the while hoping for peace.

I'd come to a conclusion. There would be no peace as long as I held onto the useless concept that God allowed Mary's death for a yet-to-be-seen glory. "And it's unacceptable that God willed my child into existence and then stood back, rather indifferent, watching me watch her die," I wrote one June day. "I know better." Even if I didn't know what the better might be, I knew that wandering around in my daughter's suicide was the only chance of finding it.

The wandering took the shape of a circle. I found myself circling around and around the incomprehensibility of suicide, trying to get light on it from different angles. The circling itself gained intelligibility when I read one day about sculptor Robert Lazzarini. An art critic in *The Washington Post* was describing the way Lazzarini fashioned ordinary objects like telephones, hammers, and violins into stretched-out distortions of the way they normally look, both recognizable and unsettling, like a Salvador Dali painting in three dimensions. Lazzarini seemed to "bend the fabric of the world," the critic wrote, "so that even our perceptions of it start to crack."[59]

Of particular interest was the response of art patrons to the work. Because there was no single viewpoint from which the telephone, hammer, and violin looked the way they ordinarily look, people kept walking around them, "trying to resolve them into some sensible whole but never quite able to figure out the spatial relationships between the parts."[60]

Suicide, I realized, bends the fabric of the world. It distorts the familiar and calls into question what we thought we knew about the people who die by it. It cracks open our perceptions of life—those dealing, in my case, with divine love and human suffering—and makes us wander around in circles, looking for sensible resolution always and everywhere, finding it oddly.

Late on a rainy April night in 2002, my mother and I were driving home from Middleburg, a nearby town, where we had seen my brother, George, play "Brandy Bottle Bates" in *Guys and Dolls*. Out from the roadside ran a white cat not ten feet from the front wheels. After a sickening bump under both front and back tires, I stopped in the road, windshield wipers clicking, wondering what to do. The nearest house was perhaps a hundred yards away. "Drive on," my mother said. "The cat's dead, and the owner might live a mile away. I know you feel bad, but there's nothing you can do."

Picturing the horror of the cat's owners at finding their crushed pet, I prayed they would piece together the truth and find some comfort. It didn't occur to me to try to find them the next day and apologize. If they were shouting, "How could you?" at faceless me, I could scarcely blame them. I had hurled the same question at my daughter, looking for answers when I most needed an apology. Those owners also deserved an apology they would never get, and I felt for them. I felt for Mary, as well. It wasn't that I placed suicide and accidental animal slaughter in the same moral category; it was that my daughter and I had both done damage, and neither of us could apologize for it. Merely imagining that Mary would want to apologize put an end to my "How could you?" questions and brought peace.

Circling dispelled anger in another way. Years before in family therapy, Jane had called suicide the ultimate angry act. That view seemed about right to me at the time, given my reflexive anger toward Mary. After John said he'd been taught the same theory in medical school, I accepted the ultimate angry act notion without question. It riled me for years.

"What was she so angry about?" I asked John. He said he didn't know.

An answer came in *The Suicidal Mind* by Edwin Shneidman, psychologist and founder of the American Association of Suicidology. Shneidman claims that profound psychological pain, or "psychache," resides at the core of almost every suicide and surfaces in suicide notes.[61] I'm certain he would have seen psychache in Mary's suicide note. I saw it myself. But I gave anger a far bigger role than I should have. According to Shneidman, suicide victims feel helpless and hopeless rather than angry, their perceptions severely constricted.

"The sad and dangerous fact," he writes, "is that in a state of constriction, the usual life-sustaining responsibilities toward loved ones are not merely disregarded . . . they are sometimes not even within the range of what is in the mind."[62] I understood that Mary wasn't able to think about her family; we were not within her thought range on the night she died. Just knowing she hadn't disregarded me erased all my anger toward her, leaving in its place new respect.

MARY, 1994.

Seven months before her death Mary wrote in her journal: "In the National Gallery of Art today, I noticed people looking at works of art in awe, wonder, curiosity, and bewilderment. But most people probably never realize that we humans are works of art made by God, far surpassing what anyone could ever put on canvas."

On some level, Mary knew herself to be a work of art made by God. That's the first truth. The second truth is that mental illness took away her ability to reason; it dehumanized and broke her. She was innocent, and she suffered unspeakably. How that hateful turn of events came about, I can't say. From the time of Job, no one has ever been able to say why the innocent suffer; only that they do. I can now say this, however: God had nothing at all to do with Mary's illness and suicide, neither causing nor allowing them, and everything to do with loving her. That's the third truth, and the day I finally believed it was one of the best days of my life.

Songs started coming to me in the morning when I woke, and I sang them as I fixed breakfast. One morning "Shall We Dance" from *The King and I* arrived from out of nowhere, and the next morning it was James Taylor's "Carolina on My Mind," followed by "A Spoonful of Sugar," "I Know That My Redeemer Liveth," "Maybe I'm Amazed," "The Lion Sleeps Tonight," and dozens more, for which most of the lyrics had to be invented since I couldn't remember the original, making John laugh. My parents used to sing in their tiny kitchen when I was young, and it never came across to me as anything but happiness.

Endnotes

45 Jessica Powers, "Prayer," *Selected Poetry of Jessica Powers*, eds. Regina Siegfried and Robert Morneau (Kansas City, MO: Sheed & Ward, 1989), 145.

46 U.S. Catholic Conference of Bishops, *Catechism of the Catholic Church* (Mahwah, NJ: Paulist Press, 1994), 550.

47 Richard J. Dillon, "Acts of the Apostles," *The New Jerome Biblical Commentary*, eds. Raymond E. Brown, S.S., Joseph A. Fitzmyer, S.J., and Roland E. Murphy, O.Carm. (Englewood Cliffs, NJ: Prentice Hall, 1990), 754.

48 St. Augustine, *Concerning the City of God against the Pagans*, trans. Henry Bettenson (London: Penguin Books, 1972), 32.

49 St. Augustine, *Essential Sermons*, ed. Daniel Doyle, O.S.A., trans. Edmund Hill, O.P. (Hyde Park, NY: New City Press, 2007), 206-7.

50 St. Thomas Aquinas, *Summa Theologiae: A Concise Translation*, ed. Timothy McDermott (Allen, TX: Christian Classics, 1989), 389.

51 Yves Congar, *The Mystery of the Church* (Baltimore, MD: Helicon Press, 1960), 110.

52 J. V. Sullivan, *Catholic Teaching on the Morality of Euthanasia* (CreateSpace Independent Publishing Platform, 2011), 50.

53 St. Thérèse of Lisieux, *St. Thérèse of Lisieux: Her Last Conversations*, trans. John Clarke, O.C.D. (Washington, DC: ICS Publications, 1977), 89.

54 St. Thérèse of Lisieux, *Story of a Soul: The Autobiography of St. Thérèse of Lisieux*, trans. John Clarke, O.C.D. (Washington, DC: ICS Publications, 1976), vii.

55 J.-M. R. Tillard, O.P., *Church of Churches: The Ecclesiology of Communion* (Collegeville, MN: The Liturgical Press, 1992), 69.

56 Pope John Paul II, "Address at Mauthausen Concentration Camp," *Origins* 18, no. 8 (July 7, 1988): 124.

57 Clarissa Pinkola Estés, *Women Who Run with the Wolves* (New York: Ballantine Books, 1995), 173.

58 Ibid.

59 Blake Gopnik, "Robert Lazzarini's Self-Tilted Works," *The Washington Post*, November 10, 2003, C-1.

60 Ibid., C-8.

61 Edwin S. Shneidman, *The Suicidal Mind* (New York: Oxford University Press, 1996), 13-5.

62 Ibid., 134.

A FINAL WORD

IN HER SUICIDE NOTE, MARY'S final request to her family was that we be gentle with one another and remember her good moments. Looking back over the years since she wrote those words, I believe we've gone some distance in meeting her request and in living the lives Mary seemed to be urging for us.

John is still practicing medicine full-time. He closed his solo practice in 2005 and now works for another internist in town. Although past retirement age, he plans to keep working as long as he can.

John Paul continues to live with John and me at our home in Manassas. His life has settled into a stable routine, and people go out of their way to tell us what a special and lovely person he has become.

Lauren is a doctoral candidate in theology at the University of Notre Dame in Indiana who now lives in Boston with her husband Andrew, an assistant professor of theology at Boston College. They share their lives with their little dog, Jubilee.

I went on to teach for five more years at the Washington Theological Union while also facilitating a bereavement support group at All Saints Parish once a year or so. Currently, I volunteer for the National Alliance on Mental Illness as a support group leader for people who have family members living with mental illness. Since 2012, I have written a blog for the suicide bereaved titled Marysshortcut.com.

John and I still go to the Carmelite monastery each month to be with our community in prayer. We celebrated forty-two years of marriage in July 2014.

My mother, Joyce, passed away on May 29, 2010, from a heart attack at the age of 89. My sister, Joy, and I were holding her hands when she took her last breath. "I'm proud of our mother," I said. "She lived her life right to the end."

Indeed, she worked until 3 p.m. the day before her death, got her hair done, and then suffered a fatal heart attack during the night. She was buried between my father and my daughter Mary, an arrangement she once told me would be perfect.

ACKNOWLEDGMENTS

THE FAMILY THAT SUSTAINED ME through the writing of this book is larger than I first realized. It naturally contains my mother, sister, and brother who told me that they knew all along I would write this account. It includes my husband, John, who offered trust and attention whenever I tried to describe a story that belongs largely to him. My son, John Paul, and daughter, Lauren, also gave quiet support by overcoming the normal misgivings of being written about and simply asking from time to time how the job was going.

There is yet another family: Our Lady of Mount Carmel community in Washington, D.C. Even though few of my Secular Discalced Carmelite friends ever knew I was working on a manuscript about Mary, the community steadied me throughout just by being what it is: a prayerful, life-giving presence.

One person generously agreed to participate in the manuscript before it was complete: Sr. Mary Ellen Black, OSB, my spiritual director, who listened as I read uneven passages for minutes at a time, a kind of paragraph babysitting only she could provide.

Several courageous people consented to read the entire, unedited manuscript as a way of helping me: author Laura Collins; Carol, editor and member of Our Lady of Mount Carmel community; Michael, my nephew; Andrew, my son-in-law; dear friends Peg and Colleen; and Fr. Joe Goldsmith, one of Mary's high school friends.

Patricia Morrison of ICS Publications contributed ongoing encouragement and Marianna McLoughlin, skillful editing and good advice.

I will always be grateful for each of you.

ABOUT THE AUTHOR

MARJORIE ANTUS, M.A. THEOLOGY, IS a wife and mother of two. She and her husband John are secular members of a Roman Catholic religious order, the Discalced Carmelites, who come together each month to pray for the needs of the church and the world.

She currently serves as an administrator for her local affiliate of the National Alliance on Mental Illness and facilitates a support group for family members of those living with mental illness. Her blog Marysshortcut.com addresses the topic of suicide bereavement.

CPSIA information can be obtained at www.ICGtesting.com
Printed in the USA
LVOW08s1204190715

446785LV00006B/775/P